How to Pick
Fund Winners

Recent MONEY *Books by Junius Ellis*

Money Adviser 1996

Investing for a Secure Retirement

Making Money With Mutual Funds

How to Pick Fund Winners

Junius Ellis
Wall Street Columnist

And the Editors of MONEY

MONEY Books
Time Inc. Home Entertainment
1271 Avenue of the Americas
New York, NY 10020

Contents

1 ■ *How to Pick Fund Winners*   7

Ways You Can Profit From This Book   9
Savor the Fab First Half of 1996   12
Prepare for More Market Vertigo   13
Don't Fall for These Fund Myths   15
Get a Grip on Your Fatso Funds   22
What Sets Fund Champs Apart   28
Gaze Beyond Morningstar's Stars   30

2 ■ *Our Market Forecast to the Year 2001*   33

Why We're Defensive Near Term   35
Funds That Win Big by Not Losing   36
Don't Fall for New Fund Phenoms   41
Small-Cap Funds With Less Risk   46
Aim to Double Your Money by 2001   48
Funds That Figure to Double   56

3 ■ *Cut Risk Without Crippling Return*   61

Key Questions to Answer Honestly   63
Plumb Your Tolerance for Pain   66
Evaluate Your Portfolio's Risk Level Now   68
Gun for Long-Term Growth   71
Fatten Your Profits Overseas   73
Angle for Both Income and Growth   75
Lock in Reliable Dividends   77
The Ideal Blend for Life's Phases   81
Tactics That Reduce Your Exposure   88

4 ■ Make Hay With Your 401(k) Funds   93

Master the Basics of Your Plan   *96*
Shield Your 401(k) From Foul Ups   *104*
Perfecting Your Plan's Fund Mix   *107*
Smart Ways to Invest Your Stash   *111*
Tap a 401(k) While You're Working   *113*
Common Mistakes You Can Avoid   *119*
Taking Money Out Once You Retire   *121*
How to Reduce Your 401(k) Tax Bill   *123*

5 ■ Manage Your Funds Like a Pro   127

Answers on Safety and Ethics   *129*
What You Don't Know About Funds   *130*
Everybody Is Flogging Funds Now   *137*
Just Say No to Gold-Plated Fees   *140*
Why You Need a Prospectus   *143*
Get to Know the Fund Manager   *144*
The Logistics of Fund Ownership   *146*
When to Abandon a Sinking Ship   *147*
Blunt the IRS' Bite of Profits   *149*
Wield Your PC to Pick Funds   *151*

6 ■ Rating Today's 25 Largest Funds   159

The 15 Largest Stock Funds   *160*
The 10 Biggest Bond Funds   *168*

Glossary   172

Index   175

1

How to Pick Fund Winners

*M*any readers of MONEY expect their standards of living to rise as their lives and careers progress. If you are in your forties or fifties, however, you could be stunned to discover when you add up your net worth that you already have amassed quite a bundle. Even if you're just starting a family, you could be surprised at your potential for accumulating some serious money. According to research by Sanford C. Bernstein, a New York City money manager, the number of people with $1 million portfolios has nearly tripled over the past 12 years. The increase in millionaires has been particularly swift in the 1990s, rising about 15% per year. The number of millionaire households was less than 1% of the population in 1989. Now it's an estimated 2.8%. Whether you aspire to or have attained such wealth, the challenge confronting you is to keep those assets growing without taking unacceptable risks.

The first step for more and more people is mutual funds, which in the 1990s have been as profitable in practice as they are sensible in theory. By pooling small investors' money to buy and sell securities on their behalf, a mutual fund provides many of the advantages once available only to the wealthy. These include professional management, diversified holdings and ready access to your cash, all at a reasonable price. The rising popularity and strong performance of funds come fortuitously at a time when many of us face difficult financial issues ahead, including job insecurity, reduced healthcare benefits and an aging Social Security system. Let's face it. The days when employers and the government provided financial security to the grave are history. These days you have to rely primarily on yourself to make sure that your family's future is adequately provided for. The question no longer is if but when and how aggressively you need to get started as a mutual fund investor.

Ways you can profit from this book. The objective of this book is to answer such questions, as precisely as possible, so that you can become a winner with funds now regardless of your age, experience or goals as an investor. Start here in Chapter 1 by checking out our analysis of recent market conditions entitled "Prepare for More Market Vertigo." Then we tell you why you shouldn't fall for some widely held fund myths; how to handle your suddenly obese fund; and what sets star fund managers apart from their many journeymen peers. Then in Chapter 2, you will find the rationale for MONEY's mostly upbeat stock and bond market forecast to the year 2001, plus recommendations of specific stock funds that figure to profit the most if our projections prove correct.

Later in Chapter 3, we'll teach you how to select funds that will help you reach your financial milestones without subjecting you to enormous risk. Our concise explanations will assist you in developing a winning strategy to achieve your goals, be they capital growth, income or a combination of the two. Then we supply model fund portfolios (see "The Ideal Blend for Life's Phases") that can be tailored to various stages of your family's financial life. In Chapter 4, you will learn everything you need to know about managing the funds in your tax-deferred 401(k) savings plan. In Chapter 5, weigh our unvarnished "Answers on Safety and Ethics" concerning those hot topics among fund investors. We also introduce you to software and services that simplify the task of tracking and picking funds. We give tips on minimizing fund expenses so that profits go into your pocket rather than the purveyors'; deciding when to sell your funds; and deploying your portfolio to keep more of your gains out of the clutches of the tax man. In Chapter 6 are our buy, sell or pass ratings on the 15 largest stock funds and 10 beefiest bond portfolios.

Study our companion fund rankings. For the latest news on your funds and any that you are interested in, you can quickly refer to MONEY's 48-page *Mutual Fund Rankings*, which accompanies this guide. There we give you a rundown of the 25 top-performing funds in six major categories. That's followed by mid-year results for 3,336 stock and bond funds. In addition to having passed their first birthday, all are open to retail investors in most states for an initial investment of $25,000 or less. Don't worry if you stumble over an unfamiliar term or strategy. Turn instead to our glossary at the end of this book. Below we also provide a quick review of the basics, whether you're a new investor or a seasoned veteran.

Bone up on the fundamentals. A mutual fund is a corporation whose sole business is to pool money from investors like you and invest it in stocks, bonds, money-market instruments or some combination of the three. When you invest in a fund, you receive shares that represent part ownership of the fund's holdings and entitle you to a proportionate slice of whatever income and profits (or losses) that those assets generate over a specified period of time. By joining forces with other investors, you enjoy a number of advantages over the do-it-yourselfers who venture into the securities markets on their own. Among the most important:

Professional management. You normally couldn't interest a professional money manager in minding your savings unless you had at least a six-figure sum to invest. With funds, however, you usually can get in the door for $1,000 to $3,000. Every fund has its own investment management team. These pros work full time tracking the markets, monitoring the fund's investments and deciding what and when to buy or sell. For these services some funds impose a sales charge, or load, on top of annual management fees and operating expenses that average 1.5% of stock funds' assets and 1% of bond funds' assets. See Chapter 5 for detailed advice on evaluating various types of fund fees.

Ample diversification. Stock funds own shares in about 90 companies, on average, while bond funds hold 70 issues. By investing in such a large number and wide range of securities, funds virtually eliminate the risk that an unforeseen plunge in the price of a single stock or bond could take a big chunk out of your money.

Access to your cash. Most mutual funds are open-ended. That means they, unlike conventional corporations, don't issue a set number of shares that trade on the stock markets or over the counter. Instead, open-ended funds issue new shares whenever you invest and buy them back whenever you cash in. Thus when you want to buy or sell, you don't have to find another investor to take the other side of the deal. That's a big plus if you invest in markets where securities trade infrequently, such as certain small-company stocks or municipal bonds.

An array of options. If the securities in the fund's portfolio appreciate, the value of your shares rises commensurately. If you redeem your shares at the higher price, you score a capital gain. You also net a gain if your fund sells some of the securities in its portfolio at a profit. Funds typically pay out all the year's net trading profits in a single capital gains distribution, usually in December. And if your fund owns bonds or other interest-bearing securities or stocks that pay dividends, the fund will also pay that income to you in the form of monthly, quarterly or semiannual income distributions. You can elect to have either kind of distribution paid to you in cash, which you might choose to do if you plan to live off the income in retirement. But if you're investing to build your wealth, you should order the fund to reinvest the distributions in additional shares.

▉ *Savor the Fab First Half of 1996*

Returns of diversified U.S. stock funds averaged almost 11% for the first six months of 1996, according to Morningstar, the data supplier for the fund rankings that accompany this book. That showing fell short of 1995's first half, when stock funds rose close to 15%. But it topped the six-month 10% rise of Standard & Poor's 500-stock index. Aggressive growth funds, which specialize in stocks smaller than those in the S&P 500, fared especially well with returns averaging 13%.

Bond investors, however, probably wish that they had skipped the first half of 1996. On January 1, long-term interest rates stood at 6%. Many forecasters expected them to drift down toward 5% by summer. Instead, a stronger than expected economy sparked inflation fears, and rates spiked as high as 7.2% before dipping just below 7% lately. As a result, the typical taxable bond fund was flat in the first six month of 1996, while its tax-free counterpart fell 0.7%. That's because bond prices fall when interest rates rise, and vice versa. High-yield bond funds managed a respectable 4.8% gain, however, largely because junk bonds often rise in value when the economy heats up.

While many funds posted impressive profits, the first half of 1996 may be remembered even more for an outbreak of fund lust. Investors poured an astonishing $125 billion into stock funds in the first six months of the year and were poised to shatter the full-year record of nearly $130 billion set in 1993. That flood of cash meant fat profits for fund companies and helped fuel the industry's boom in mergers and acquisitions. In the month of June alone, famed value investor Michael Price sold Heine Securities, which manages the Mutual Series funds, to Franklin Resources for $610 million. Morgan Stanley snapped up Van Kampen/American Capital for $745 million. And industry giant Merrill Lynch paid about $200 million to add Hotchkis & Wiley to its fund portfolio.

Prepare for More Market Vertigo

The stock market's swoon started in early July when some high-profile companies began reporting disappointing profits for the second quarter of 1996. In the following weeks, the Dow Jones industrial average fell about 7%. High-technology stocks were hit hardest, plunging more than 15%. Share prices could suffer further seizures over the next six to 12 months. MONEY believes it's likely that the Dow, lately 5670, will fall below the 5000 mark, down more than 15% from its 1996 peak of nearly 5780. But we don't anticipate a recession that would trigger an extended bear market. Instead, we expect that stocks will resume rising within a year. Thus the best conservative strategy is to take advantage of stock market rallies to sell fund holdings that make you nervous and reinvest the proceeds in lower-risk stock funds such as those discussed in Chapter 2, "Our Market Forecast to the Year 2001."

Gyrations in stocks will continue. Attentive investors were heartened by Alan Greenspan's July testimony before the Senate and House Banking Committees. The usually evasive Federal Reserve chairman, America's chief economist, all but predicted that economic growth would slow from the recent annual rate of roughly 4% to about 2% next year without a recession. Inflation, he said, would remain 3% or less through 1997. Greenspan also acknowledged that if the economy started expanding fast enough to push inflation substantially above 3%, the Fed would consider raising short-term interest rates to help rein in the growth.

Here's the bottom line for investors. Stock prices could slump whether the economy slackens on its own or with the Fed's help. But they would rebound once growth has eased enough to allow long-term interest rates to fall a percentage point to 6% or so. This upbeat outlook has just one catch, which Greenspan himself noted. The placid stock market conditions for most of the past five years have been an exception. So investors should brace for more sharp market swings in the year ahead.

Investor psychology has changed. The chief problem for the stock market is that corporate profit growth has dropped off sharply. The July stock sell-off began when Motorola reported net income for the second quarter had dropped 32% from year-earlier levels. The company's shares promptly fell 15%, kicking off a broad decline in technology stocks. The effect of disappointing earnings reports could be magnified because small investors now play an enormous role in the stock market through mutual funds. The bull market of the past few years was pumped up by the hundreds of billions of dollars of new cash that cascaded into stock funds.

The flood of cash into stock funds crested earlier this year at an average of nearly $25 billion a month. Once investors became concerned about companies' earnings, the flow slowed to $14 billion in June and an estimated $7 billion in July. This drop in fund inflows probably won't last long, however. The baby boom generation has buckets of cash to invest and few attractive places to stash it. In addition, there's little historic evidence that jittery stock prices make small investors withdraw money from stock funds for long. Investors are almost certain to start piling into funds again, reigniting the bull market, as soon as the current corporate earnings downturn is over and fears of higher interest rates have passed.

Why interest rates are crucial. Rising interest rates are poison for the stock market. An increase of one percentage point in long-term rates knocks down the underlying value of blue-chip stocks by about 15%. Stock prices don't always reflect that erosion of value right away. But they usually respond within nine months or so. Interest rates' recent one-point rise to around 7% would justify a 15% drop in the Dow from its 1996 high near 5780. Moreover, if rates remain high for the next six months and corporate profits start declining, damage to the Dow could conceivably be as much as 20%, knocking the average below 4700.

MONEY doesn't think interest rates will remain high for that long. Rates are already high enough to slow economic activity sharply before the end of the year. Once the economy slows, long-term bond yields could start coming down. Long-term rates ultimately could fall as much as a full percentage point. That would rekindle a powerful bull market in stocks, setting the Dow on course for 9000 by the year 2001. In addition, bond prices would soar. If rates decline one point over the next 12 months, 30-year Treasury bonds could return nearly 20% including both price gains and interest.

Don't Fall for These Fund Myths

It's interesting how many people invest in funds without really questioning the numerous assumptions, sayings and pseudostatistics that, over time, have achieved almost mythical status. While the conventional wisdom isn't always wrong, it's seldom as wise as it might seem. Put another way, there's a world of difference between good advice and advice that sounds good. And today's fund myths can lead you astray because they all sound compelling. That's part of the problem. They seem so simple and clear that you want to believe them. Here in rough order of their popularity are the nominees for the 10 costliest fund myths, each with a lesson to make you a smarter investor.

Myth 1: Hot funds can also give you scorching long-term results. You would probably dismiss as naive someone who predicted that a baseball team will win the next World Series because they won last year's. So why would you think a fund will finish on top in 1996 simply because it had a hot 1995? These days not many folks remember Oppenheimer Ninety-

Ten Fund. It was the top performer of 1987, with a 94% return. But this hot fund doesn't even exist anymore. In 1991, Ninety-Ten was absorbed into Oppenheimer Asset Allocation. Similarly, the Oppenheimer Global Biotech Fund skyrocketed 121% in 1991, then lost 23% the next year and was swallowed up by Oppenheimer Global Emerging Growth Fund in 1994.

History is full of flash-in-the-pan funds underscoring the fact that short-term performance is not a reliable guide to the long-term future. Study after study proves it. Yet the *Journal of Financial Planning*, published by the Institute of Certified Financial Planners, actually has recommended buying the funds with the hottest returns over the past 30 days. If you're not convinced of the fallacy of buying last year's sizzlers, ask yourself what you gain by chasing performance. The answer is a bigger tax bill unless you fling your hot funds around in a retirement account. Ask your accountant what your combined federal, state and local tax bracket is. Say it's 38%. That means your churning basket of hot funds has to outperform an S&P 500 index fund by more than 38% a year just to stay even with it after tax.

Myth 2: Focus on performance and forget small stuff like expenses. Brokers and fund executives like to say that investors pay too much attention to annual expenses and too little to performance. In fact, investors pay far too much heed to performance and not nearly enough to expenses. Here's why costs matter. A fund's annual operating expense (or expense ratio, in fundspeak) is reported as a percentage of total net assets. That keeps it looking small, usually under 2%. On a $1,000 investment, 2% in expenses eats up just $20 a year. But if your fund earns 20%, that 2% expense ratio eats up a tenth of your return. In other words, the fund company really charged you 10% in expenses, not 2%. Decades ago, funds routinely reported their expenses as a percentage of investment income so you could see how big the bite really was. These days, you have to do the math yourself.

If, say, the long-term return on stocks after all taxes and inflation works out to less than 4%, even a fund that reports just 1% in expenses will devour at least a quarter of your take-home return. And over time, the average low-expense fund is certain to outperform the average high-expense fund. Thus you shouldn't buy an investment-grade bond fund with expenses above 1% of net assets (for junk bond funds, 1.25% is the limit). Don't buy a U.S. stock fund with expenses higher than 1.5%. You might go a little higher if you want to own a small-cap fund. Don't buy an international fund with expenses above 2%. Hundreds of terrific funds easily pass those tests.

Myth 3: The more funds you own in your portfolio, the better.

Many financial planners recommend that you hold well over a dozen funds at once to spread your risks. Get real. You simply don't need duplicate funds with the same investment objectives, such as long-term growth. True, some growth managers buy classic earnings-driven shares while others go for out-of-favor value plays. But many of their holdings will be remarkably similar. Thus more funds may not be better. Our advice? In both your taxable and tax-deferred accounts like IRAs and 401(k)s, start with a large-stock fund such as an S&P 500 index fund. Then add a diversified international stock fund in both your taxable and tax-deferred caches. If your federal tax bracket is 28% or higher, you should put a municipal bond fund in your taxable account. Put a junk bond fund or an intermediate-term (not a long-term) Treasury fund in your retirement account, where its yield won't bloat your tax bill. One money-market fund is plenty. If you don't own any hard assets like a house, you might also consider an inflation-hedging fund (discussed in detail later).

Myth 4: If you want to score big, load up on small-cap funds.

According to oft-cited numbers from research firm Ibbotson Associates, small stocks have beaten big stocks by two percentage points a year since 1926. Why? Small stocks, says the conventional wisdom, are inefficient. That means they are so rarely studied by Wall Street analysts and the investing public that bargains abound. Not true, says small-cap pioneer Charles Royce, who runs $1.7 billion in little stocks at the Royce Funds in New York City. "The mythology says small-caps are so inherently inefficient that they're like automatic gold in the streets," explains Royce. "Ten years ago, that was true. But I couldn't look anyone in the face today and say small-caps are inefficient—not with so many funds out there, not when any investor can instantly get the same information on any small company." Another problem is that for most of the past 70 years, the big returns from those small stocks were produced by the littlest 20% of companies (measured by total market value) on the New York Stock Exchange. Fair enough. But those shares aren't the same stocks favored by today's small-cap managers.

Consider that the grandaddy of all small-cappers, T. Rowe Price New Horizons, has outperformed big stock funds by only about a percentage point per year on average since its inception in 1960. That's about the biggest edge you can expect, and much of it was earned in the 1970s. If you really want to capture any possible small-cap advantage, put some of your assets in a microcap fund specializing in true midget stocks. You also should be prepared to ride with the fund for up to five years. It may take that long for the stocks' values to be realized.

Myth 5: Aggressive growth funds will push your portfolio higher. This myth is a cousin to Myth No. 1. Imagine *Smart Money* magazine exclaiming: "A $1,000 annual investment getting a 20% return in an aggressive growth fund will leave you with $224,026 in 20 years." The math is okay, but the logic isn't. To begin with, no aggressive growth fund in existence has averaged 20% annually for the past 20 years. Unless you expect a titanic bull market over the next two decades, this isn't even a myth. It's sheer fantasy. Since January 1976, according to calculations by Morningstar, aggressive growth funds have returned 17% annually, beating the stock market by 2.5 percentage points per year. But most experts don't think 1976 is a good place to start counting. That's because stocks were just nosing up from the worst dive since 1929. The riskiest funds may have got the biggest lift in the bull market that followed.

Go back deeper in time, and the case for aggressive growth is weaker. Take a look at Lipper Analytical Services' data on capital appreciation and small-company funds, two aggressive investing styles, dating back 25 years. Small-company funds did perform a tad better than plain old growth funds, rising by 13% a year, vs. 12%. But capital appreciation funds fell behind by a hair, gaining 11% annually. Neither number proves that aggressive growth pays off in the long run. Our advice? Put the bulk of your long-term money in a conventional growth fund, not in one dubbed aggressive.

Myth 6: Investing in junk bond funds is playing a sucker's game. The memory of 1989 and 1990, when many junk bond funds lost a quarter of their value, is painfully fresh. From 1985 to 1994, however, junk bonds delivered roughly the same 12.5% annual return as long-term Treasury bonds at barely one-third of the risk. That's because bonds issued by young or financially feeble firms pay higher interest than do Treasuries. Thus they return more money to you sooner, thereby shielding you better from the damage of rising interest rates. In judicious measure, junk bonds are a defensible long-term investment and are far less risky than most people believe. They are usually not suitable for taxable accounts, however, because their high current income will hike your tax bill. Hold them instead in tax-deferred accounts like 401(k)s.

Myth 7: As an inflation hedge, stash some money in gold funds. Gold itself has proved a worthy inflation beater over time. Its price gains, according to Ibbotson Associates, have outpaced rises in the consumer price index, especially in times of high inflation. But understand this about investing in gold funds. They don't always have the mettle of the metal itself. Over the past 10 years, gold prices averaged a piddly 1.7% annual increase. But two leading gold funds, United Services Gold Shares and Lexington Strategic Investments, lost 16% and 5% of their value, respectively. That's because gold funds don't usually buy bullion. They buy the stocks of companies that run gold mines or related businesses, which may not always be as good as gold. So if you want to hedge against inflation, buy a house in a stable neighborhood of a growing community. Or consider T. Rowe Price New Era, which holds a basket of inflation-busting assets like timber, mining, and oil and gas stocks.

Myth 8: You can transform a load fund into a no-load these days.
Many brokers are pushing so-called class B or class C shares of load funds as alternatives to old-fashioned front-end loads. Brokers often refer to these weird alphabet funds as no-loads. Fact is, a load is a load, whether you pay your broker's commission in one lump up front or in, say, 1% increments for several years (as you customarily do with the B or C shares). Don't get fooled. These B or C shares still charge loads. And they can end up costing more than the original front-end load if you hold them for five years or longer. A 5% front-end load, spread over a five-year holding period, is 1% annually. Many alphabet funds keep charging that much for six years or even more. Under a new National Association of Securities Dealers rule, brokers must discuss which form of fund sales charge is most suitable for a customer like you. If your broker fails to explain the different ways you can pay, get a new broker. Better yet, pay your broker the old-fashioned way, via an up-front load. One load-fund family that has said no to alphabet soup is the American Funds group of Los Angeles.

Myth 9: Wherever you live, own a muni fund that's double tax-free.
Residents of several states with no income tax, like Florida, Texas and Washington,

can buy municipal bond funds that offer tax-free bonds from within the state. So what? Every other state's muni bonds are also tax-free if you live in those three states. Why buy an in-state fund with a sales load or a high expense ratio when you can get a national muni fund with identical tax benefits from low-cost providers like Benham, Fidelity, Safeco, Scudder, USAA or Vanguard? Even in states that do have an income tax, you'll often be better off with a low-expense national muni fund than with one that's double tax-free. That's because the extra expenses on the in-state fund tend to gobble up your tax savings. What's more, how do you know you won't be moving to a new state? Your old Kentucky muni fund won't do much for you if you relocate to Arizona. Unless you live in a very high-tax state like California, Massachusetts or New York, skip double tax-free and go for a national muni fund instead.

Myth 10: International funds greatly broaden your profit horizons. Back in 1993, a sluggish year for U.S. stocks, investors put a record $40 billion in funds that invest abroad. That year international funds shot up 39%, on average, and U.S. investors thought they had found paradise. Look again. In 1994, international funds lost 3%. Last year, as U.S. funds earned 30% returns, international funds rose a measly 5%. Perhaps too many of 1993's buyers didn't understand that the performance of foreign stocks is partly driven by the value of the U.S. dollar. When you put $1,000 into an international fund, you are selling a thousand greenbacks and buying a basket of pounds, French francs, German marks, Japanese yen, Dutch guilders or Indian rupees. That's because the fund has to exchange your dollars into francs and yen to buy stocks denominated in those currencies.

If these other currencies later rise in value against the buck, your fund will get a boost because its foreign holdings can be converted back into more U.S. dollars. Since 1985, the U.S. dollar has slumped against other currencies. Over the past decade, Morgan Stanley Capital

International's index of European and Asian stocks returned 12% annually. Nearly half of that handsome return came from the fall of the U.S. dollar. If the dollar reverses its long decline, international stocks may not perform as well as they did in the past decade.

Get a Grip on Your Fatso Funds

There's one aspect of today's stampede into funds that is troubling—bigger is not always better. For investors, it's often worse. When funds puff up, they can be transformed almost beyond recognition. New and existing shareholders may be relying on a very different fund than they think. Moreover, since sponsors get richer as funds get fatter, the fund industry has no incentive to correct the problem.

To see how rapid asset growth can transform funds, we consulted the fund trackers at Morningstar. We zeroed in on two groups of diversified U.S. stock funds. Each of the 102 funds in the first group had assets of $100 million or less at the end of 1990 as well as at the start of 1996. We'll call them the petite funds. The 15 funds in the second group also started out with no more than $100 million. But each bulked up to $1 billion or more by the start of this year. We'll call them the fatso funds. The average market value of the stocks in the petite portfolios rose 58% (from $4 billion to $6.3 billion), well under the 92% hike in the S&P 500's average stock value. But the size of the fatso funds' typical stock shot up 209% (from $2 billion to $6.1 billion). The fatsos started out owning far smaller stocks than the petites but ended up owning stocks nearly as big.

Big funds have to buy bigger stocks. Look at Twentieth Century Ultra, lately with total assets of nearly $18 billion. In 1990 it had just $458 million spread across 62 stocks. That's an average of $7.4 million in each. Such small stakes can easily be bought or sold on the open market with little effect on the prices even of tiny stocks.

In 1996, however, Ultra had to invest well over $100 million per stock. If Ultra tried to buy or sell such huge blocks of small stocks, it could singlehandedly throw supply and demand out of whack, raising the price it pays to buy or depressing the price it gets on sales. That's called market impact, and it can wreck a fund's performance. One way to skirt the problem is to buy bigger stocks with greater aggregate market values. Today the market value of Ultra's stocks averages $6.6 billion, more than 10 times larger than in 1990. Explains Ultra president James Stowers: "As hard as we try, there's no way we can buy stocks as small as we used to. We have to buy bigger stocks to put all the money to work." Then he adds: "Sometimes we wish we were smaller. It would be a lot easier job, and the returns might be higher too."

Or consider the Oakmark Fund. Launched in 1991, it had $328 million at the end of 1992. Manager Robert Sanborn had 10% of his assets in small stock Liberty Media while it rose thirteenfold from 1991 to 1993. But Oakmark recently had assets of $4 billion. So there's no way Sanborn can cram 10% of the fund, or about $400 million, into one small stock, no matter how dazzling its prospects. The result? "Embedded in the fund," says Sanborn, "is a much higher percentage of the S&P 500 than there was two or three years ago." Beating the market by loading up on small stocks like Liberty is a lot harder for big Oakmark than it was for little Oakmark.

Big funds have to buy more stocks. From 1990 to 1996, the average number of stocks owned by the petite funds rose 55%, to 71. At the fatso funds, the average number of stocks rose 212%, to 176. Why did the faster-growing funds buy so many more stocks? When a lot of money comes in, the manager is compelled to invest it. Otherwise, he will depress his results in rising markets like that of the past five years. Most likely, he buys a growing number of stocks that are less familiar to him than his old favorites.

Look at PBHG Growth, which shot up from $12 million in assets in 1990 to $4.8 billion lately. "I can't honestly say the fund is no different from when it was at $50 million," says manager Gary Pilgrim. "You need a wider span of attention when you own 130 stocks than when you owned 60." Common sense suggests that the hottest fund managers are getting stretched thin. Even if they've added to their staff of analysts, how can they know all these new stocks as well as they did their old ones? And if these new stocks are such bargains, why didn't the fund own little bites of them when it was smaller? Truth is, petite funds tend to own a few stocks their managers really love. Fatso funds end up owning too many stocks the managers merely like.

Big funds buy pricier stocks. In 1990, our group of petite funds owned stocks whose price-earnings ratios averaged 16. By 1995, their PEs averaged nearly 23, or 43% higher. But the fatso funds started out with a PE of almost 18 and ended up at 26, or 47% higher. By comparison, the market's PE rose only 27% to 20. So the faster funds grow, the more they buy pricier, riskier stocks than they used to. Why? There simply aren't enough good stocks on sale at any one time to absorb all the fresh cash. Check out Alliance Growth. In 1990, the PEs of its stocks averaged 12, or 23% below the market's. At the start of 1996, the fund's PE averaged roughly 25, or 20% higher than the market's.

Big funds won't continue to excel. The fatso funds have so far performed well under these new burdens. From 1990 to 1996, reckons Morningstar, the fatsos returned 26% annually, vs. just 13% for the petites. So what's the rub? This tidal wave of money is so new that it hasn't yet had time to do much damage. But it will. There are already unmistakable signs of the troubles to come. Over the past decade, a host of funds have slipped from market beaters to market laggards after pushing past $1 billion in assets. Among them are Evergreen Total Return, Janus Venture, Berger 100, Dreyfus Growth & Income and Vista Growth & Income. Also look to history. In 1968, the hot go-go funds sucked in billions of dollars almost overnight. Enterprise Fund, for example, took in some $600 million in 1968 (the equivalent to $2.6 billion now) thanks to its 118% return in 1967. But much of that new cash was sunk into the second-rate stocks then available. As a result, Enterprise lost 45% of its value in 1969 and 1970.

William Sams, who now runs FPA Paramount Fund, joined Enterprise to help clean up the mess in 1969. What was it like? "Money was coming in at $6 million a day. There was even a machine with a readout showing how many callers couldn't get through by the end of the day." Sams laughs but then adds soberly: "The funds today have the same kind of cash inflows. I think we've got another speculative binge in the making now. It scares me to death." This influx of cash also highlights the fact that you and your fund manager have ultimately conflicting interests. You make the most money when the fund reaches its optimum asset size and sticks to it. But the fund manager makes money by collecting fees. The larger a fund gets, the more fees it pays the manager regardless of how well it does for you.

Big funds have conflicts of interest. Think of your fund manager as a real estate developer and your fund as a new house in the woods. Once you move in, you don't want other people crowding in and spoiling your view. But it's the rare developer who agrees with you. He wants to sell as many houses as he possibly can. Harvard finance professor André Perold and noted money manager R.S. Salomon summed up this paradox in an article called "The Right Amount of Assets Under Management" in the *Financial Analysts Journal* five years ago. They explained that every money manager's success carries the seeds of failure. The more unusual the manager's approach was when he was small, the higher the odds that it will become unsustainable as his funds grow. Concluded Perold and Salomon: "A firm's first client should be unhappy to see other clients sign on…as new accounts are added, wealth created per client declines." By encouraging floods of new money

to pour into their portfolios, today's fund managers may be jeopardizing the future returns of existing customers.

Consider the Kaufmann Fund, which lately had $4.3 billion in assets, up from a mere $40 million at the end of 1990. The fund's average market value is now three times bigger ($547 million vs. $164 million), and it owns eight times as many stocks (294 vs. 35). In 1995, after four straight years of walloping the stock market by as much as 49 percentage points a year, it slipped behind the S&P 500 slightly (36.7% vs. 37.5%). Is Kaufmann too big? "I don't think it's any harder [to run the fund] at this size," notes co-manager Lawrence Auriana. He says that recent computer advances allow him and partner Hans Utsch to pick stocks as effectively as when the fund was small. Says Auriana: "The management is still the same. We're good stock pickers." What's more, he adds, "we're satisfied with our results." So are his shareholders, who have earned a fat 25% annually over the past five years.

MONEY, however, thinks Auriana and Utsch are endangering their returns, while enriching themselves, by continuing to solicit new shareholders with ads and direct mail financed by current shareholders. Like three out of five stock funds, Kaufmann charges its shareholders an annual 12b-1 marketing fee (in this case, 0.6%) to pay for advertising. On the assets they've attracted this way, Auriana and Utsch's company will collect annual management fees of $51 million. Auriana doesn't agree. "The only people who are unhappy with the 12b-1 fee are the ones who didn't invest in the fund," he says flatly.

Huge Magellan should trim its sails. What about the No. 1 fatso, Fidelity Magellan, with assets of $55 billion? As discussed in detail in Chapter 6, new manager Robert Stansky moved into the fund's hot seat vacated in May when Jeff Vinik suddenly quit after four years of running Magellan. We think Magellan is too big to sustain its great long-term returns and should close to new investors so that it won't become even more unwieldy. Don't hold your breath. At last count, Magellan alone generated $423 million a year in management fees for sponsor Fidelity.

The fund family has other gushers too. When the firm launched its New Millennium Fund in 1992, its marketing guide pledged that "the fund will limit its assets to $500 million." In November 1995, the top-performing fund blew past $500 million and kept on growing. When pressed about the written pledge in the marketing guide, Fidelity's Roger Servison counters that it was not in "a legally binding document" and points out that New Millennium's binding prospectus made no such promise.

Fidelity is hardly alone in its eagerness to take in more money than clients expected. In April 1995, Gary Pilgrim closed his $1.1 billion PBHG Growth Fund to new investors "to maintain the highest level of performance for our shareholders." The fund had grown from just $3 million at the end of 1992. Then, in January 1996, the fund reopened. Pilgrim explains that he's added enough staff to handle the extra money. But he admits that his institutional small-cap account, which he closed at the same time, remains shuttered. "The pension consultants [for institutional investors] are more strict about these things," he explains.

How investors can protect themselves.
There has always been a potential conflict of interest between the people who own the fund and the people who own the fund's management company. In fact, the first draft of the Investment Company Act of 1940, the law that governs mutual funds, barred any fund from taking in new money once it hit $150 million in assets. That's equivalent to $1.6 billion today, an amount that seems almost quaint now. The drafters of the bill feared that "too large an aggregation of capital could not be efficiently managed." The final law omitted the $150 million limit. But it did empower the Securities and Exchange Commission to review whether funds are getting too big for their customers' good. The last time the SEC looked at the issue was some 30 years ago. Then only nine funds had more than $1 billion in assets apiece. Still, the SEC warned in a report to Congress: "Should the growth of the largest funds and fund complexes continue, these

What Sets Fund Champs Apart From Their Peers

Nobody follows mutual funds more intensely than Ken Gregory in Orinda, Calif. Gregory edits a well-respected monthly newsletter, *No-Load Fund Analyst*, that provides commentary on more than 100 funds ($225 a year; 800-776-9555). He and partner Craig Litman also manage $300 million in assets at their firm, Litman/Gregory & Co. Here are the attributes that Gregory thinks separate great fund managers from mere journeymen.

■ **Who are the superstar managers?** There are six managing no-load funds. There is Hakan Castegren of Harbor International, which invests in foreign stocks. Unfortunately, the fund is closed to new investors. But Castegren follows the same strategy with Ivy International (5.75% load). Another is Michael Price, who has a group of funds with Mutual in their name. There's also Dick Weiss of the Strong Opportunity fund; Foster Friess of Brandywine; Shelby Davis of Selected American Shares; and Mason Hawkins of Longleaf Partners, which is closed to new investors. But Hawkins' Longleaf Partners Small Cap follows an identical approach, only with smaller outfits.

■ **What makes these guys stars?** They all have great performance over 10 years or more, either with their current funds or at others before that. They also share important character traits including the ability to learn from their mistakes, a passion for their work and independent thinking. Take Dick Weiss. There's a lot of original thought going on below the surface. He knows that everyone on Wall Street uses PE ratios to figure a stock's value. So he uses a system he developed during his early years as an analyst. He figures what the private market value of a company is, taking into account its cash flow and growth rate, among other things, and then buys the stock only when it's trading at a 20% to 40% discount to this value. He avoids overpaying for stocks because his numbers tell him what a company is really worth. He refuses to get caught up in Wall Street's hype.

■ **Do all have a disciplined approach?** Yes, though what they are disciplined about varies. For example, Mason Hawkins is a classic value investor. But he doesn't look just for cheap stocks. Instead, he buys businesses in which he wants to be a partner with management, as he puts it. That means he has to understand the industry. If he doesn't comprehend how the business works, he can't judge the viability of management's plans for the company and he won't buy the stock. This rule means that he doesn't invest in biotechnology or precious-metals outfits even when they are prospering. He sticks to his knitting.

■ **What if that approach falls out of favor?** Any manager worth his salt will have periods of poor performance. But it's smart to remain patient with these folks. From 1989 to 1991, Michael Price's Mutual Shares fund delivered terrible returns. He earned a total of 26%, trailing our value composite benchmark by about 15 points. Over the next three years, however, Price earned more than 53%, nearly doubling the benchmark. The moral is simple. It pays to stay put unless there's clear evidence that something has changed dramatically at a fund such as a marked increase in money under management or turnover in staff.

■ **What other traits do stars share?** They all try to limit their risk. Michael Price, Mason Hawkins and Dick Weiss measure value according to their own methodology and buy only shares that are selling at sizable discounts to their assessment. Even Foster Friess, who invests in much more volatile growth stocks, manages risk by investing only when he thinks he understands a company better than Wall Street does. To make sure a company he owns isn't headed for an earnings disappointment, Friess keeps a checklist of 24 things to watch out for, including whether earnings growth is primarily due to accounting changes and whether inventory is growing faster than sales. It's worth noting, however, that aversion to risk doesn't keep these stars from making big bets in specific sectors or stocks. Shelby Davis has had close to 50% of his fund in financial companies, while Hakan Castegren has had about 10% in South African companies.

■ **Who are the rising stars?** I've been really impressed with Robert Sanborn, who runs the Oakmark fund. Oakmark looks for undiscovered value in small and mid-cap U.S. stocks. In fact, Oakmark is one of the few funds that didn't have a five-year record when I recommended it. It's clear that Sanborn has a burning passion for the business and the confidence to act on his convictions even when Wall Street doesn't agree. Another stock picker with promise is Jim Goff, who runs Janus Enterprise, a small-cap growth fund. Goff doesn't have a five-year record with the fund either. But he's a research maniac. He knows his companies inside and out. When he has an idea he likes, he's not afraid to make a big bet on it. If I have confidence in a manager, I like to see him run a concentrated portfolio—that is, take big positions in a smaller number of stocks. I figure there are a limited number of great ideas out there, so why dilute them with a bunch of second-tier picks? Both Sanborn and Goff tend to run concentrated portfolios.

funds might soon reach the point where their portfolio mobility would be so seriously impaired as to affect gravely the interests of their shareholders."

Your best defense is to think small. Don't buy funds whose assets, say, have at least doubled or grown by $1 billion or more over the past year. Also stick with outfits that have shown they know when to stop taking in money. Among them are Longleaf Partners, Quantitative Numeric, Royce, T. Rowe Price, Vanguard and Wasatch. Another tip is to lean toward funds whose managers put their own money in them. (This information is often found in the footnotes to the financial statements in fund annual reports.) As Longleaf's Mason Hawkins explains: "Our employees have more than $60 million of our own capital in the funds. We're not driven by fees but by compounding our own capital. We did not want more money. Investing is difficult enough without having to do things that are irrational—like buying second-rate stocks just to put extra cash to work."

Don't hesitate to take action. Say you own a fund that has grown very big, very fast. You should write the fund company, as well as the fund's board of directors, and demand that no more new customers be brought into the fund against your best interests. If the directors are up for election on a proxy, vote to fire them. And keep your expectations in check. Many hot funds today can no longer maintain the nimble portfolios that made them famous. Your hot fund's returns are likely to be more sluggish, and risk may well be higher, now that it has grown so large. If that bothers you, think about selling your fund and putting the proceeds into a fund that is not raking in assets as fast. You may have to give up a little performance in the short run. But in the long run you will likely come out ahead.

Gaze Beyond Morningstar's Stars

The top five-star rating from fund ranker Morningstar has become synonymous with success. Indeed, about

87% of all new money invested in U.S. stock funds goes into those rated four or five stars by Morningstar. This statistic suggests that too many investors are using Morningstar as the ultimate shortcut. They basically count the stars and buy the fund. As if this star-crossed tactic weren't rampant enough, soon you'll be seeing even more stars. Morningstar announced this year that it will begin providing one-year star ratings in addition to its scores over three, five and 10 years. The step was taken to enable funds to comply with advertising rules set by the National Association of Securities Dealers.

With at least 9,000 funds from which to choose, investors can be forgiven for feeling they need a handy screening tool. But the star system is a clumsy one at best. The folks at Morningstar say as much themselves. "We've consistently conceded the limitations of our star ratings," says president Don Phillips. "The star rating is not a conclusion. It's a starting point." Both Phillips and Morningstar publisher John Rekenthaler say they've owned several one-star funds and that the bulk of their assets are in funds with three or four stars.

How fund stars are born. A look at this process will help explain the shortcomings of the star system. Morningstar computes each fund's total return and its risk (the average amount by which the fund underperforms the short-term Treasury bill). It then subtracts any sales loads and compares each fund's figures with the average of all funds in its broad category. These are stock, hybrid (which includes funds that own both stocks and bonds), taxable bond or tax-free bond. Morningstar divides the resulting range of scores into five tiers. The top 10% of funds in each category land in the highest tier, winning five stars. The next 22.5% form the second tier, earning four stars. The following 35% get three stars. And the remainder get one or two stars.

There are several flaws in this scheme. First, the stars tell you quite a bit about a fund's past but very little about its future. Stars also tend to tell you more about fund categories than about individual funds. A remarkable 52% of all U.S. aggressive growth funds recently had four or five stars. All this really says is that the sector is booming. In contrast, only 5% of foreign funds lately carried four or five stars, down from 31% at the end of 1994. But the slump merely reflects the fact that the U.S. market has been stronger than the vast majority of foreign ones. That's because Morningstar rates foreign funds against all stock funds (most of which invest in companies based in the U.S.). Likewise, Morningstar compares short-term and long-term bond funds on the same scale even though they react very differently to changes in interest rates. Phillips defends the broad rating scales, saying that extra refinements would simply cause other distortions. In the future, however, users of the firm's software may be able to customize their own fund baskets for star ratings.

How best to evaluate stars. For openers, ignore the new one-year rating altogether. The period is too short to tell you anything useful. Even before counting stars over a longer period, ask whether a fund owns U.S. or foreign, large or small, low-priced or high-priced stocks? Does a bond fund favor short term or long term, investment grade or junk? Does it overlap with funds you already own? How much did it lose in the market drops of 1987 and 1990? Do its average returns come mainly from one or two great years or from steadily good results? Are its expenses low? Does it generate a high or low income tax bill? The wealth of data available from Morningstar (plus services from Lipper Analytical, Value Line and MONEY itself) can help you answer these vital questions. Only after you've narrowed your search to worthy candidates should you look to the stars to help you make a final choice.

Morningstar's Rekenthaler suggests that investors use the stars to determine which fund asset categories are in favor and which are not. Depending on your tolerance for risk, you may want to buy a fund in a hot asset class on the gamble that it will stay sizzling. Or you might bet on a cold one in hopes that it will soon defrost.

2

Our Market Forecast to The Year 2001

*D*uring Senate debate prior to the June 20 confirmation of Alan Greenspan as the chairman of the Federal Reserve, one critical senator called him "a human brake pad," for holding back the economy to reduce inflation. But most of the others agreed with Senator Alfonse D'Amato. He described Greenspan as a superstar who should be allowed to continue his nine-year war against inflation. "Greenspan will do whatever he thinks is necessary to win the fight," says economist Bruce Steinberg at Merrill Lynch. "But he may not have to do much because inflation is so well-behaved." Economist Edward Yardeni at Deutsche Morgan Grenfell/C.J. Lawrence agrees. "Inflation is going to head even lower," he predicts. Both commodity prices and wholesale prices are falling, Yardeni explains, and that means smaller increases in consumer prices are ahead.

MONEY thinks a slowdown in the economy later this year could restrain inflation even more. One reason is that interest rates have already reached levels high enough to discourage business activity. "Bond yields have risen more than a percentage point since the beginning of 1996," says Steinberg. "Historically, when you've seen an increase of that size, the economy has never failed to slow." A softer economy could hurt the stock market by undermining corporate profits. Such weakness has already started cropping up among small, high-tech growth stocks. But a sluggish economy also could help bring down long-term interest rates by a full percentage point over the next 12 months, triggering a boom in bond prices and the stock market as well.

Why we're defensive near term. "Bonds are likely to beat stocks over the next 12 months," says Steve Leuthold of the Leuthold Group, a Minneapolis investment advisory firm. We agree. In fact, the outlook for long-term bonds is the best it's been for more than a year. Here's our analysis. We see the economy slowing from its recent 4% real, or inflation-adjusted, growth rate to only 2% in 1997. Furthermore, we expect that inflation won't get much worse than its recent rate of less than 3% a year. As a result, yields on long-term bonds (and funds specializing in them) could sink from today's nearly 7% to as low as 6% within a year. That rate decline would produce total returns of as much as 20% on long-term issues.

The 30 Dow stocks, lately 5670, increasingly look as though they are poised for a temporary 15% to 18% drop to as low as 4700 before year-end. As the economy softens, investors are likely to start worrying that corporate profits are going to fall short of analysts' estimates and mark down share prices. "Slower earnings gains could turn the stock market's tail winds into head winds," says economist Kathryn Lunstrum at Duff & Phelps in Chicago. The tip-off that a stock market pullback may be close is the increasing volatility of share prices in recent months. "Volatility tends to be low in a strong, rising stock market," says Leuthold, who has analyzed the stock market's daily ups and downs over the past 100 years. In fact, the stock market's daily swings from 1992 to 1996 were less than half the historic average. Lately, however, daily fluctuations in stock prices have doubled. "If volatility keeps going up, that would be a sign that we're getting close to a market top," says Leuthold.

Thus this is a time to restrict any new investments in stock funds to conservative choices (see "Funds That Win Big by Not Losing" below). High on our list are income-minded stock funds that favor companies likely to boost their dividends. Stocks that pay solid dividends tend to bounce around less than growth investments do. As you sell some of your past winners, don't feel you have to reinvest all your profits in stock funds. Consider putting some money into 30-year Treasuries and corresponding long-term bond funds that hold such topnotch issues. In short, fortify your asset mix with bigger holdings of long-term bonds and other income investments such as high-yield stocks. That will help you keep your overall portfolio on track to a double-digit return even if the stock market takes a nasty 15% tumble in the coming months.

Why we're bullish longer term. Our cautious stance on the Dow over the next 12 months or so does not change the fact that the long-term prospects for stocks remain enticing. Among the reasons are the enormous underlying strength of the U.S. economy and the fact that aging baby boomers are continuing to sock away more than $20 billion a month in stock funds. Moreover, if you make wise choices now and resist the temptation to flee the market at the first signs of trouble, you can look forward to another blockbuster stock boom in the late 1990s. The brutal cost cutting of the past decade has turned many U.S. companies into money machines. Once the stock market has retreated 15% and the economy is securely on the path of sustainable growth with low inflation, the Dow has the potential to double to around 9000 by the year 2001. We present our rationale, as well as stock funds that seem destined to profit from it, later in this chapter.

Funds That Win Big by Not Losing

If MONEY's cautious market forecast is correct, stock funds as a group will be lucky to make money over the coming year. But that doesn't mean you should abandon stocks for those dowdy wallflowers called CDs and money-market funds. Long-term investors usually are better off remaining in stocks, particularly since we think the Dow could double by the year 2001. While those comfy cash instruments would protect you against any losses, chances are you'd get caught looking for your dancing shoes when the market strikes up again. Missing the start of a rally can be costly. Let's say you were smart enough to bail out of stocks just before the market's last major decline, when the S&P 500 fell 15% from June through October 1990. If you didn't anticipate the bull market's resumption, you would have missed the most powerful upturn in a terrific year for stocks. The index rose 31% in 1991, with half of the gain occurring in the first quarter. By contrast, if you had simply stayed put in stocks through the full 19 months of downs and ups between June 1990 and January 1992, you would have finished with a 22% profit. And you would have avoided any commissions and taxes on transactions.

To help you get through the next year with minimal discomfort and maximum profit, we focused on stock funds that aim to limit risk over those that go all out for big gains. If the market tanks, funds whose strategy is to sidestep trouble will outperform those that chase trendy stocks and sectors. So we searched for Steady Eddies that deliver solid returns with little volatility. That's because risk is more predictable than is performance. A hot performer may cool off. But a fund that has been less volatile than the norm is likely to remain so.

To find funds that win by not losing, MONEY asked Morningstar to divide its database of diversified U.S. stock funds into five categories of investment style. We sorted large-company funds, which buy stocks with market values over $5 billion, into three groups. Growth funds buy stocks with rapidly rising earnings. Value funds seek out-of-favor stocks worth more than the market recognizes. And blended funds mix both styles. Our two other categories were funds that hold mid-size companies (market values of $1 billion to $5 billion) and ones that buy small firms (under $1 billion).

We then isolated the funds that ranked in the top 20% of each category over a recent five-year period. From that high-performing group, we looked for funds with standard deviations below their category's average.

Standard deviation, a common risk measurement, indicates the degree to which a fund's returns bounce up and down from month to month. (Lower numbers signify steadier returns.) We eliminated all the funds that produced a 20% or greater loss in any single quarter and ones that have had recent management changes. Then, out of the remaining candidates, we chose the fund in each style category with the lowest standard deviation. Here are the five Steady Eddies that we selected.

Fidelity Equity Income II. This large-company value portfolio is the Clark Kent of stock funds. It is mild mannered on the surface but able to leap over the S&P 500 benchmark. During the past five years, the fund has racked up a super return of almost 19% annually. How? Manager Brian Posner shockproofs his portfolio by keeping 80% of assets in dividend-paying stocks. The steady income from these securities helps support their prices when the market falters. But Posner isn't interested in a company just because its dividend is high or its stock price is low. "I try to avoid the value trap of buying companies simply because they're cheap," he says. Instead, he looks for companies making changes that he believes will improve earnings or cash flow. Posner, who has run the fund since April 1992, has found many such buys in the financial sector, including American Express. Other favorites include energy stocks like British Petroleum and Schlumberger. Unlike some of his Fidelity colleagues, Posner has largely avoided high-flying technology stocks.

Mutual Beacon. You may have read that famed value investor Michael Price has sold Beacon and three other funds (Mutual Shares, Mutual Discovery and Mutual Qualified) to Franklin. But investors who like Mike can rest easy that he will remain at the helm for at least five years. "I want to find stocks that might go down two points but are more likely to go up 20," Price says. While he applies that formula to all his funds, Beacon came out on top in our search with a five-year return of 18% annually that was 40% less volatile than the norm. Price fills this portfolio with an eclectic assortment of offbeat companies, small stocks, bankruptcies and merger candidates. For example, Price owned 2 million shares of defense manufacturer Loral, which announced a merger with Lockheed in a deal worth $44 a share. That was a 25% premium over Loral's trading price. Price will continue to hold the stock after the deal is completed. "Loral alone is worth $38," says Price, "So at $44, you're getting all of Lockheed for just $6 a share, and it's worth $10 or $11." Not content to wait until the market gets around to recognizing the values he unearths, Price will occasionally turn activist. Last year he bought 6% of Chase Manhattan to become the bank's biggest shareholder. Price then pushed publicly for Chase management to merge with Chemical Bank—a deal that helped Chase's stock price double in 1995. Price feels the stock will continue to climb as the cost-cutting benefits of the merger kick in.

Princor Growth. Co-managers Michael Hamilton and Gary Craven combine the "bottom up" and "top down" investing approaches in running this large-company growth fund. In making choices for their portfolio, they first analyze blue-chip companies to find those with solid balance sheets and good management. Then they apply a macroeconomic forecast to pinpoint the sectors of the economy that are likely to grow fastest over the next three to five years. "We try to buy the strongest companies in the strongest sectors," says Hamilton, manager since 1987. Craven came on board as co-manager in 1991. This two-pronged attack has clearly proved profitable for Princor Growth, whose A shares have chalked up a market-beating return of 16% annually over the past five years.

The team has found the most opportunities in the healthcare sector, which they believe will benefit from the aging of the baby-boom population. "Once you cross over age 40, your need for health care increases geometrically," says Hamilton. For the past two years, they have been repeat buyers of medical companies such as Boston Scientific, a producer of catheter and angioplasty devices. They also have owned managed care providers such as Foundation Health, United Healthcare and FHP International. Another big bet has been technology, including Microsoft. Hamilton reasons that demand for computer gear can only increase as businesses strive to pare costs and improve efficiency. He and Craven foresee a temporary economic slow-down over the next year or so. So they are stashing holdings in so-called growth cyclicals—companies with products that are tied to the business cycle but generate steady earnings growth.

T. Rowe Price Equity Income. Its 16% annual return over the past five years can best be summed up in one word—dividends. Manager Brian Rogers aims for a portfolio yield that is 25% above the S&P 500's. To create this rich income stream, Rogers favors stocks whose yields are at a relative high compared with their historic payouts. He then scans the underlying balance sheets to be certain the companies can sustain those payouts. This focus on unusually high dividends not only helps keep risk down. It also directs Rogers to temporarily out-of-favor stocks—often growth issues that rebound profitably. "This fund is a recycling facility for other people's underperformers," he says. For example, he was a big buyer of drug companies after the 1993 health reform scare knocked down their prices by about 30% (and boosted their dividend yields to 4% to 5%). He recently sold his stakes in Merck and Pfizer after they notched 50% to 60% gains and their dividend yields dropped by about a third. The fund also holds a big stake in energy firms. "Oil stocks have held up well when the market has been weak," Rogers says. Recently he has been adding cyclical stocks—economically sensitive companies like papermakers Georgia Pacific and Union Camp plus chemical giant Du Pont.

Third Avenue Value. Manager Martin Whitman, age 71, says he has no plans to retire from a fund that he's run since October 1990. Still, he's not taking any chances.

He works with a team of eight analysts, two of whom he's grooming as successors. He tries not to take any chances with his stock and bond picks either. Although he traffics in volatile small companies, Whitman says, "I want them safe and cheap." For Whitman, safety means companies with strong balance sheets and solid management that are in businesses he feels confident analyzing, such as banking and insurance. Cheap means stocks selling at half of what he estimates an acquirer would pay for the entire company. This disciplined strategy has paid off handsomely for Third Avenue, which has gained 16% annually over the past five years.

Stocks make up about 65% of the portfolio. Nearly half recently was invested in financial firms, such as banks. Whitman hopes to cash in on the merger and takeover wave sweeping the industry. His holdings have included Financial Securities Assurance, a credit insurance company, and First American Financial, a title insurer. His search for undervalued issues has also steered him to technology. Tech shares are volatile, he concedes, "but the values are there." When it comes to managing the fund's bond stake, Whitman looks for severely depressed bonds paying "at least five percentage points more than comparable issues," he says. Such a premium, of course, usually means the issuer is in trouble. Whitman doesn't worry. He carefully checks the issuer's balance sheet to make sure it has enough assets to cover its senior debt in the event of a bankruptcy. Then he buys the bonds that stand first in line for repayment. For example, he has snapped up $40 million worth of BB-rated K Mart bonds that he believes will be paid in full whether or not the company goes under.

Don't Fall for New Fund Phenoms

If you like to scan the fund performance tables in your newspaper, you've probably noticed that many brand-new entries have posted big returns. The first thing to realize is that many of these debutants concentrate on narrow, overlapping market niches such as small company and aggressive growth. That's no accident. Those two sectors have been hot lately, and success draws a crowd. Says Robert Puff, chief investment officer at the Twentieth Century funds: "The industry collectively will keep introducing whatever has been working well." And how. Since the beginning of 1995, nearly 100 small-cap and aggressive growth funds have been launched.

Meanwhile, Wall Street has rolled out record volumes of initial public offerings (IPOs), or stocks sold to the public for the first time. IPOs are the high-octane fuel of small-cap and aggressive growth funds. The result is a magical money launching pad. The new funds buy hot little stocks, making them hotter, driving up the funds' returns, attracting more money to the funds, heating up their favorite stocks further—and drawing more IPOs to market. Beyond that, new funds have some natural advantages over their older rivals. It just so happens that small-cap and aggressive growth portfolios tend to get the biggest boost from most of them. Consider:

New funds invariably are smaller. The bigger a fund gets, the more likely its performance is to slow down as it swells up with a greater number of bigger stocks at higher prices. But funds are born small. By law, a fund must open for business with a maximum of 25 investors, who usually pony up a total of $100,000 to $1,000,000. When customers pour $10 million of new money into a $1 billion stock fund, that's just a 1% cash inflow. But another $10 million at a $10 million fund is a 100% cash inflow. "If new cash is a very high percentage of total assets," says Ronald Baron of the Baron funds, "you can keep applying large sums into your best ideas."

Their managers are hungrier. Explains David Testa of T. Rowe Price: "When you take a highly motivated individual, back him with substantial resources and give him a portfolio to call his own, the intensity of effort is something to behold." Funds generally don't make money for the management company until they take in about $200 million. So attracting assets with high performance right off the bat is the name of the game.

New entries get plenty of TLC. "New pools of money always get the firm's fresh ideas," says Gary Pilgrim of PBHG Growth Fund. Why? Partly it's just human nature. Asks Michael Price of the Mutual Series funds: "Do you have kids? Who gets the most attention, the oldest or the baby?" Sure, Price's comment is self-interested; he wants lots of customers for his baby fund. But he has a point about tender loving care. Ever heard of "incubator funds"? Back in the 1960s, money managers would start a bunch of funds and run them in secret for a few years. Later they would terminate the flops and trot out the surviving boffo funds for the public to buy. The records of the lousy funds disappeared, making the firms seem better managers than they really were. Nobody admits doing this today. But the practice is commonplace. One reason new funds do so well is that, by incubating them, the money managers know they have hatched a winner before they announce its birth.

Another form of TLC is "bootstrapping." That means the newest fund in a family gets first crack at a hot little stock. Then the firm's older, bigger funds pile into the stock, driving up the price and boosting the new fund's return. There's nothing inherently unethical about boot-strapping. But you need to bear it in mind when you evaluate the long-term skill of a new fund manager. What's more, bootstrapping gives the biggest bang for the buck in a market that's rich in IPOs. Says Puff of Twentieth Century: "If there's an interesting IPO, maybe we can get 50,000 shares total. If it's a $20 stock, that's $1 million. In a $15 billion fund, $1 million is too small to make an impact. But in a new fund it could make a big difference. So we would allocate the IPO shares where they would make the biggest difference, given the charters of the funds."

Their managers have lots of cash. Wayne Wagner of Plexus Group, a consulting firm in Santa

Monica, found in a study that the typical fund manager's buy decision added 0.7% to the fund's short-term return. But the sell decision subtracted 1.1%. Why? As natural optimists, fund managers are better at sensing when a stock is improving than when it is decaying. And selling a weakening stock can hurt the price further. Thus the manager of a new fund, whose fresh cash makes him a constant buyer, has better odds of outperforming a bull market. Baby funds can buy a lot faster. "If a manager gets a new idea that we think should be a 2% holding in our funds," says PBHG's Pilgrim, "it might take 500,000 shares to get to that level in $4.8 billion PBHG Growth. That could take a week. But one of our new funds might need only 15,000 shares for a 2% position, and that might take only half a day." This speed works best at aggressive growth and small-company funds that pile into stocks whose prices are rising fast. It doesn't help much at large-company or value-minded funds.

How to size up today's hotshots. Aggressive

young funds have a lot going for them in a bull market. After nearly 15 years of mostly up markets, however, you're a lot more likely to be buying a new fund near a peak than near the bottom. Remember too that new fund managers tend to be bright young folks who've never been through a real bear market. Their magic may suddenly stop working when stock prices stop rising. And the advantage could well revert to more experienced managers. Thus the best use for new funds is as a place to put your mad money—the spare change you're willing to gamble with. There's nothing wrong with gambling a little as long as you understand that's exactly what you're doing. New funds are a high-risk bet. Don't let anyone tell you otherwise. If you can't afford to lose at least half of what you're putting in, you shouldn't even think about it. Here are some guidelines to keep in mind when buying a new fund.

Favor names that you know. Some big fund families with strong track records seem to have unusually powerful launching pads. Their new funds often beat the averages by 10 percentage points or more in their first year. But the fund industry overall is full of fizzles. According to the fund raters at Morningstar, of the roughly 550 diversified U.S. stock funds introduced since the end of 1990, just half have beaten their older peers in their first year. In other words, your odds of success are just fifty-fifty. That's why it makes sense to favor new funds from the biggest families, or from managers with long-term records at older funds.

■ **Stick with your overall strategy.** You should never buy any fund just because it's new. Instead, you should first decide which category of fund you may need to add to your portfolio. Then weigh the alternatives. Thus if you've been thinking that you need more international exposure, you might consider buying a new Europe fund. But if you already own plenty of small-cap and aggressive growth funds, don't bloat your portfolio with more of them.

■ **Keep your expectations realistic.** Garrett Van Wagoner racked up an amazing 55% annual return over nearly three years at his earlier fund, Govett Smaller Companies. His new Van Wagoner Emerging Growth fund was up 50% in just the first half of 1996. If you think he can keep doing this much longer, you are destined to be disappointed. New investors often assume that much of Van Wagoner's success comes from his skill. But much of it also comes from his being in the right place at the right time. And make sure you can take the heat. Managers of fast-growing funds have learned that many new customers sign on if big risks pay off, while few sell if the risks end up losing money, according to research by professors Erik Sirri of Babson College and Peter Tufano of Harvard. Thus the managers can be tempted to go for broke. And if the market stumbles, new funds in high-flying categories like small-cap growth are likely to come crashing to earth. Take Oberweis Emerging Growth, which was launched in January 1987.

In that year's October crash, the fund nosedived more than 40%, or nearly twice the overall market's swoon.

◼ *Small-Cap Funds With Less Risk*

Analysts expect earnings at smaller companies (those whose total share value is below $1 billion) to jump nearly 30% in 1996. That's about triple the 10% gain predicted for the large firms in the S&P 500 index, according to IBES International, a securities data firm. Before you seek profits in these tiny powerhouses, be aware that small-stock funds as a group are about 20% more volatile than are stock funds overall. To make your foray into these fetching funds as safe as possible, we opted to screen the Morningstar database for small-cap specialists. We started with those whose performance has beaten the Russell 2000 index of smaller companies as well as their fund category over the past 12 months and three years while compiling below-average risk scores. We eliminated funds that have had management changes in the past three years. The remaining funds with the best combinations of risk and reward are profiled below. The latest data on performance and expenses can be found in the fund rankings that accompany this guide.

Baron Asset. Manager Ron Baron has kept his fund about 25% less risky than the typical stock fund by largely shunning volatile technology stocks But Baron is no Luddite. "I avoid computer, semiconductor and software makers because it's tough to tell whether their products will be in demand over my investment horizon of three to five years," he explains. "Instead, I look for companies that use technology to make themselves or their clients more efficient and have the potential to grow at least 50% over two years." Such standouts in his portfolio have included $412 million (recent market value) Flextronics, which assembles modems and other products for various manufacturers, and $407 million Learning Tree, which trains corporate employees to use new technology.

Franklin Small Cap Growth. Fund manager Ed Jamieson guards against big losses by filling up his portfolio with fast-growing companies whose price-earnings ratios haven't shot through the roof. Says Jamieson: "If a stock has a PE of 20, for instance, I try to make sure that the company can grow its earnings by at least 20% a year for the foreseeable future." His hunt for bargain-priced growth lately has led him to build a position in foreign firms whose shares are selling at lower prices than similar U.S. companies. Examples have included $214 million Fulcrum Technologies, a Canadian maker of information-management software.

SunAmerica Small Company Growth. Manager Audrey Snell vanquishes volatility by committing no more than 1% to 2% of her assets to any one stock. "I try to identify trends, like the aging of the population in most countries, then look for industries that will be positively affected by those trends," she says. "So I'll bet on sectors. But I don't make big bets on stocks." Snell has been tilting toward healthcare, technology and service companies. Her favorite healthcare plays have included two drugmakers, $445 million Neurex and $210 million Guilford Pharmaceuticals, with promising new products under development.

Warburg Pincus Emerging Growth. Sufficient diversification is the watchword of co-managers Beth Dater and Steve Lurito. Although more than 30% of their money has been devoted to tech stocks of all stripes, they also have had sizable holdings in the service, healthcare and energy sectors. Lurito thinks the little-publicized energy field has much more going for it than the recent run-up in oil prices. "There's a big revolution going on," he says. "It's being driven by new computer applications that help drillers discover oil more efficiently." One firm in their portfolio that stands to profit from that trend is Petroleum Geo-Services, a $805 million Norwegian company that surveys potential drilling sites in the North Sea using three-dimensional seismic equipment.

Aim to Double Your Money by 2001

The torrent of cash pouring into stock funds has recently slowed. But corporate profits continue to climb. As a result, MONEY thinks the Dow could nearly double, topping 9000, by the year 2001. Of course, no stock market advance goes on forever without a hitch. A confidence-shaking 15% to 20% setback for stock prices sometime soon now appears more and more likely. When stocks gain more than 20% in a calendar year, as was the case last year, they frequently post a loss the following year. Since last fall, MONEY has predicted that stocks would suffer a decline of 15% or more. But that decline would likely be followed by another major surge in share prices and stock funds over the next five years.

While corporate profits will likely rise over the rest of the decade, they could disappoint shareholders this year. "The pattern of earnings reports has been deteriorating," says Paine Webber analyst Thomas Doerflinger. He notes that for last year's fourth quarter, almost twice as many earnings reports were below what shareholders expected than were above. Just the reverse was true when the current stock boom was revving up in the fourth quarter of 1994. But now the economy seems destined to slow to the point that MONEY sees growth of only 2% next year. Once the slowdown is past, we expect economic expansion to resume. Here's why.

Demographic trends favor stock funds. The first of 78 million baby boomers turn 50 this year and will represent the cutting edge of the U.S. population for the next decade or longer. As the population ages, the number of Americans ages 50 to 54 will soar to more than 17 million by 2001, up from fewer than 11 million in the mid-1980s (see the chart at right). These middle-aged Americans know all too well that they are far less financially prepared for retirement than their parents were. One reason is that traditional pensions and Social Security are likely to cover a smaller and smaller slice of retirement costs. Retirees in the next century will have to

A Surge of Savings Will Drive the Dow

The oldest baby boomers started turning 50 this year. As a growing number of Americans (beige) enter their peak earnings years, they'll pour more and more cash (green) into retirement investment plans such as 401(k)s. That rising tide of cash could power the Dow (red) above 9000 by 2001.

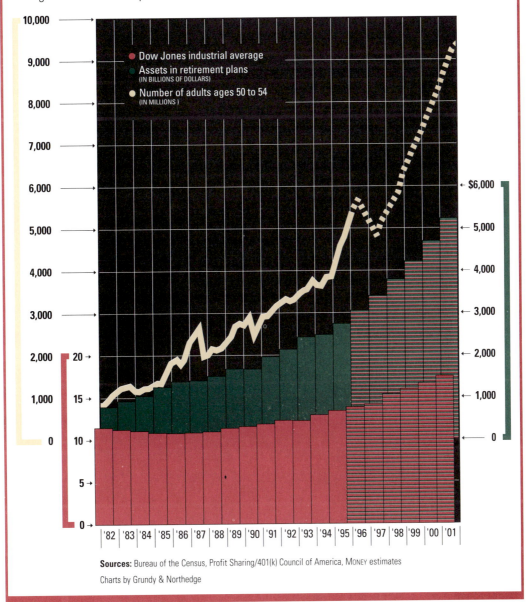

- ● Dow Jones industrial average
- ● Assets in retirement plans
  (IN BILLIONS OF DOLLARS)
- ● Number of adults ages 50 to 54
  (IN MILLIONS)

Sources: Bureau of the Census, Profit Sharing/401(k) Council of America, MONEY estimates

Charts by Grundy & Northedge

depend increasingly on contributions to tax-deferred retirement plans, such as 401(k)s, and other investments.

Economists frequently claim that we are lousy savers, citing the fact that Americans spend all but 4¢ of every after-tax dollar we earn. But that 4% savings rate masks a boom in middle-class savings. As a group, the poorer half of the American population is saving little or actually "dissaving" by running up bigger and bigger credit-card debts. By contrast, the more affluent half of the population is socking away as much as 10% of after-tax income, or thousands of dollars a year.

As a consequence, billions of dollars are now being funneled into stock funds through retirement accounts. "The participation rate of workers who qualify for 401(k) plans recently soared to an estimated 75%, up from 57% in 1988," says economist Edward Yardeni at Deutsche Morgan Grenfell. Indeed, by 2001 the total assets in retirement accounts are projected to climb from just over $3 trillion today to more than $5 trillion. And roughly half of all new contributions are going into stocks and stock funds. As a result, the flow of cash into stock funds has swollen to more than $100 billion annually (see the top chart at right).

This coming flood of money is chasing fewer stocks as big companies consolidate. During the late 1980s, more than $400 billion of stock disappeared from the market as corporate mergers and stock buybacks reduced the total amount of shares outstanding (see the bottom chart at right). In the early 1990s, the dollar amount of stock increased thanks to a boom in new stock offerings. Last year, however, mergers and buybacks again shrank the supply. The result of this trend is easy to predict. When more cash starts chasing fewer shares of stock, you get higher prices for stocks and stock funds.

Corporate profits should keep climbing. The rush of cash alone would not be able to keep share prices aloft without a boost from business fundamentals as well. Fortunately, that support exists. The wind that's behind the current bull market has been an enormous

More and More Cash is Chasing Fewer Stocks

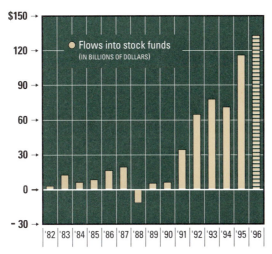

Flows into stock funds
(IN BILLIONS OF DOLLARS)

Sources: Investment Company Institute, MONEY estimates

Roughly half of all retirement savings goes into stock mutual funds, directly or through savings plans such as 401(k)s. Total inflows topped the $100 billion mark in 1995, and 1996 contributions figure to be even larger (see the chart above). At the same time, the amount of stock outstanding is shrinking. From 1991 through 1994, new issues more than made up for shares withdrawn from the market through buybacks and mergers (see the chart below). But since 1994, more stock has been removed from the market than added. When you increase demand and shrink supply for any commodity, including stocks, you invariably get higher prices.

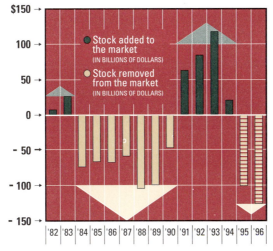

Stock added to the market
(IN BILLIONS OF DOLLARS)

Stock removed from the market
(IN BILLIONS OF DOLLARS)

Sources: Bank Credit Analyst Publications, Leuthold Group, MONEY estimates

Low Inflation Will Hold Down Interest Rates

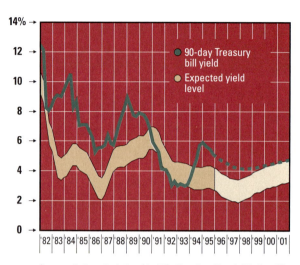

Sources: Business Statistics of the U.S., Bloomberg Financial Markets, MONEY estimates

Flat or declining interest rates help to preserve the bull market. Cheap money enables companies to keep investing heavily, boosting earnings. The two charts project short- and long-term yields (green line in top chart; red line in bottom chart) based on the levels a simple economic model predicts they would be (beige bands). Normal yields for Treasury bills are inflation over the previous 12 months plus a real return of up to 1.5%. Bond yields reflect average inflation over four years plus a real return of 2% to 3.5%.

Sources: Bloomberg Financial Markets, MONEY estimates

Rising Corporate Profits Will Boost the Dow

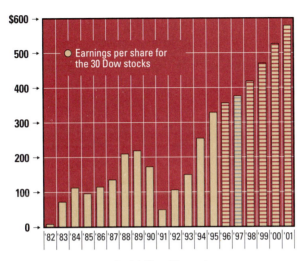

● Earnings per share for the 30 Dow stocks

Sources: Investment Dealer's Digest, MONEY estimates

The average earnings per share for the 30 Dow stocks (see the chart above) could rise more than 60% over the next five years. We project blue-chip stocks will trade at price-earnings ratios (see the chart below) averaging around 16 in 2001. If our projections are on the money, the Dow could comfortably top 9000.

● Typical stock price-earnings ratios

Sources: Prudential Securities, MONEY estimates

gain in companies' earnings, reinforced by a sharp 50% decline in interest rates since 1982. Corporate profits have nearly quadrupled since 1982. Extensive capital spending has made U.S. firms far more competitive. Combined with ongoing cost cutting, those capital investments have boosted the profitability of U.S. companies at a brisk rate (see the chart at right). As a result, pretax profits have soared from $160 billion in 1982 to an estimated $600 billion this year.

Most of the recent gains in stock prices have come from strong earnings growth. When the bull market began in 1982, price-earnings ratios for large, established companies averaged as low as 7. By 1992, the average PE had doubled to 15. Thus much of the stock market's gain during those 10 years came from rising PEs. Since 1992, however, PEs have risen very little on average. Over most of the past four years, earnings growth by itself has been strong enough to keep share prices on the upswing.

Earnings will resume their rapid growth once the current economic slowdown is past. Indeed, we believe corporate profits will rise powerfully over the next five years. "Because of cost cutting, downsizing and extensive capital spending, U.S. industry is more competitive than it has been at any time since the 1960s," says Joseph McAlinden, chief investment officer at Dean Witter Intercapital. The result will be another spurt of profit increases. And as investors become convinced that strong earnings growth need not drive up today's low inflation, we expect that the market will rebound from any temporary slump and renew its powerful advance.

Flat labor costs undermine inflation. The current bull market has benefited enormously from this century's sharpest decline in interest rates. Since 1982, inflation has fallen by two-thirds and interest rates have been cut in half. Such a drop in rates typically leads to higher earnings multiples as companies' future earnings become relatively more valuable. Inflation worries appear to be behind us, however. "Last year's 2.5% inflation rate was the lowest since 1986, and the rate is dropping," says Ed

New Investment Propels Firms' Profits

Increased capital spending (represented by the bars below) has made U.S. companies more efficient—and enormously more profitable. Since 1982, corporations have invested trillions of dollars in technology and restructuring their operations. The payoff? U.S. firms are more competitive than they have been at any time since the 1960s. As a result, corporate profits (red area) have almost quadrupled over the past 14 years.

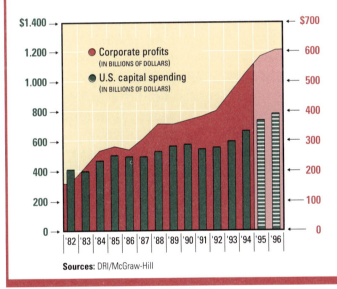

Sources: DRI/McGraw-Hill

Yardeni. One reason is that labor costs are nearly flat. Wages and benefits rose a scant 2.9% in 1995, the smallest gain since 1982. Low inflation, in turn, will keep interest rates in check. Shortly before Federal Reserve chairman Alan Greenspan's appointment for another four-year term, he told Congress that he might cut interest rates again this year. "If we envisage that inflationary pressures are significantly subdued, it would not be inconsistent to move rates lower," said Greenspan.

Earnings growth will accelerate in '98. With the economy showing signs of a slowdown that could continue for 12 months, companies are likely to report profit gains averaging only 6% to 8% this year and next. Once the slowdown is over, that growth rate will rise to 10% to 12% a year. At that pace, earnings per share for the typical Dow stock could easily rise over 60% by 2001. Furthermore, stocks still are not perilously overpriced relative to today's low rate of inflation. We expect average PEs for large companies to rise above 16 over the next five years. If earnings for the Dow stocks climb over 60%, as we predict, share prices could jump 70% on average. That would put the Dow above 9000 by 2001.

Funds That Figure to Double

Fund fans can play for doubles by following the strategy we've just outlined and considering the five funds profiled below. Heading our list is Vanguard Index–Growth in keeping with our belief that some of your stock fund investment should be committed to an index fund that mimics the holdings, and thus performance, of a broad basket of large-cap stocks. The fund owns the fastest-growing stocks in the S&P 500 index. We also suggest four actively managed funds that have shown a consistent ability to beat the market.

In general, indexing is prudent when investing in the kind of large, brand-name stocks we expect to outrun the market over the next five years. That's because these widely held powerhouse companies like Coca-Cola and Gillette are so thoroughly scrutinized by investment analysts that it's hard for even the shrewdest stock pickers to get an edge. Among the more than 300 large-company stock funds with five-year records, only 89 beat the 16% annual gain of the S&P 500 index over a recent five-year stretch. So just one of four funds topped the broad market average. By contrast, emerging markets or very small U.S. stocks provide greater opportunities for skilled managers to strut their stuff. Still, our research led us to funds that break away from the pack even in the heavily trafficked large-stock arena. We found these standouts by screening the Morningstar database for large-company funds in the top third of their investment category for the past one, three and five years. We also insisted that their managers have at least a four-year tenure. We then sized up those hardy survivors to see whose strategy seemed most in tune with the themes detailed in MONEY's long-range forecast.

Each of the stalwarts profiled here is well positioned to post the 15% annualized gains that are needed to double your money by 2001. While that's a lot to expect of any investment, it's not as though we're asking them to do something they've never done before. All four managed funds delivered doubles over recent five-year periods, returning 17% to 20% annually vs. 15% for the S&P 500. (Vanguard Index–Growth has only been in existence for three years.) We describe our choices in detail below, starting with the index fund. The latest data on performance and expenses can be found in the fund rankings that accompany this guide.

Vanguard Index–Growth. It concentrates on the fastest-growing stocks in the S&P index by tracking the S&P/Barra Growth index. Barra, a Berkeley quantitative consulting firm, divides the 500 stocks in the S&P index into "growth" and "value" camps on the basis of price to book value. This key ratio expresses a stock's price as a multiple of the per-share value of the firm's net worth. Barra considers the price-book ratio the most reliable way to identify high-growth stocks because other measures, such as price-earnings, are more easily distorted by short-term changes in a company's operations. Barra assigns high PB stocks to the growth index and low PB stocks to its value index, making sure that both camps have equal aggregate market value (current stock price times the total shares outstanding). The 163 stocks with the highest PB ratios are in the growth index. The other 337 issues are in the value index and corresponding Vanguard Index–Value fund.

Growth has been golden for the past two years. Index–Growth gained 38% in 1995 and 3% in 1994, beating out Value's advance of 37% in 1995 and its 0.7%

loss in 1994. That's not to say Growth always wins. In 1993, Value buried Growth, 18% to 2%. For the next five years or so, however, MONEY expects the stocks in the Growth portfolio to be the best index approach to doubling your money. Manager Gus Sauter says prospective Index–Growth investors should be prepared to stomach about 5% to 10% more risk than the S&P 500's.

Harbor Capital Appreciation. Manager Spiros (Sig) Segalas has had about 40% of his assets plugged into technology issues for the past year. Recent holdings included Intel, Hewlett-Packard and Cisco Systems. The penchant for high-tech reflects Segalas' insistence that his stocks have potential earnings growth double or triple the 7% historical rate of the S&P 500. "Today, it's hard to find that type of growth outside of technology," he says. And he is confident that demand for sophisticated computer gear won't short out. "In a world where there is virtually no inflation, companies can't grow simply by increasing their prices," says the 30-year investing veteran. "Other than layoffs," he adds, "using technology to increase productivity is the way to keep up profits." But he is quick to point out that his stake is spread over three different industry segments that don't always move in sync. They are computer systems, networking and software.

Beyond the wired world, Segalas has had 18% of the fund in consumer staples, including such deep blue chips as McDonald's and Coca-Cola, as well as 16% in healthcare stocks such as Merck. "The portfolio may be volatile over the short term. But it isn't risky in the sense of not being diversified," says Segalas. In fact, the fund was only 7% more volatile than the typical growth fund during the past three years and 10% riskier over the previous five years, according to a proprietary measure compiled by Morningstar. (The calculation measures how often and by how much a fund's average monthly return underperforms the riskless return of 90-day U.S. Treasury bills.) But investors were compensated for that risk. The fund's return during those two periods topped that of stock funds overall by 46% and 37%, respectively.

Davis New York Venture. No matter how you slice the pie, the fund's one-year, three-year, five-year, 10-year and even 15-year returns rank among the top 20% of growth funds. Shelby Davis, who has run the fund since its 1969 launch, selected his son Chris in early 1995 to be co-manager. "Dad is the 60-year-old brain making the big-picture calls," says Chris, "and I'm the 30-year-old legs visiting all the companies." Father and son prefer to buy undervalued growth stocks before the rest of the market discovers them and their prices start to soar. Lately, that has meant avoiding frenzied technology stocks (about 10% of the portfolio). Instead, Davis has been adding to his financial services holdings (50% of assets). Financial stocks have been a cornerstone of Davis New York Venture for many years. The roster has included American Express, Dean Witter, Morgan Stanley and Travelers.

Last year's sharp decline in long-term interest rates from 8% to 6% boosted financials and helped power the fund to a 42% gain, vs. 32% for the typical growth portfolio. Yet Chris Davis isn't cashing in his big winners. Although he believes financials have finished their sharp rebound from the banking recession of the early 1990s, he still contends they have room to grow. "Financials are a great example of one of our favorite investing themes, namely stocks that the market thinks are cyclical, but we see as merely volatile," says Davis. "Sure, return on equity may be up 20% one year, then rise just 13% the next year, and then reach up to 17% the following year. The point is that over the long term these firms are consistently growing. That's what we want."

Neuberger & Berman Focus. Like the Davises, co-managers Larry Marx and Kent Simons say they have an appetite for growth stocks only when they can be bought on the cheap. "There's a misperception that we value guys don't want growth," says Marx. "We want it just as much as those growth guys. It's just that we won't pay any price for it." Indeed, the portfolio's average PE ratio of 12 is well below Vanguard Index–Growth's 18.

At the same time, Focus sports a projected earnings growth rate of 17%, vs. about 14% for the Vanguard fund. About 70% of the fund's assets lately were invested in large and mid-size firms, with the biggest concentration a 30% wager on financial services stocks, such as Citicorp, Federal National Mortgage Association and Wells Fargo. Recently the managers have added credit-card issuers First USA and MBNA to their flock of financials. "Wall Street has dumped on all credit-card companies because of a general concern that the delinquency rate for consumer payments is rising," says Marx. "What we see is dominant firms that know how to manage losses, and they have earnings growth of 20% that we paid just 11 or 12 times earnings to buy."

IDS New Dimensions.

In addition to doing his own numbers crunching, New Dimensions manager Gordon Fines taps into the U.S. stock research staff at IDS to find firms that can reliably deliver annual earnings gains of at least 15%. As you would expect, that quest for rapid growth often leads him to technology stocks. About one quarter of his fund's assets has been invested in the computer and telecommunications industries. Among Fines' biggest holdings were familiar names such as Cisco Systems, Hewlett-Packard and Microsoft. In addition to tech, Fines is tuned into healthcare issues. About 13% of the portfolio has been in pharmaceutical giants such as Johnson & Johnson, Merck and Pfizer as well as biotech leader Amgen. These stocks have been on a roll lately. But Fines thinks they have plenty of profits in their future and isn't letting them go. "I let my winners continue to run as long as they continue to meet our earnings expectations," he says. With 75% of assets invested in S&P 500 issues, the portfolio is replete with other household names such as McDonald's, Coca-Cola, and Procter & Gamble. In other words, just the sort of solid blue chips that we believe have the best shot at leading the stock market's march into the next century, propelling New Dimensions and the four other funds we've featured to double your money by 2001.

Cut Risk Without Crippling Return

*S*ay that you possess the discipline to save $500 a month for 30 years and put it all in a riskless money-market fund. If your money earns roughly 6.5% annually, on average, you would accumulate about $553,000. Now let's say that you put your money instead into a growth-minded mix of mostly stock funds and some bond funds. Assuming an average return approaching 10% a year, an achievable one for such a portfolio over three decades, you would end up with a cool $1 million bundle. The price for nearly doubling your return, however, would be much greater uncertainty in the short run. With only a moderately risky growth portfolio, you still should be prepared to ride out market drops that could be as grim as 20% in the course of several months or even weeks.

Whether you are starting or unscrambling your nest egg, you should be able to manage your money confidently by following the investing strategies outlined in this chapter. The key decisions in the years ahead will hinge mainly on how old you are, where your financial assets are concentrated, your outlook for the economy and your tolerance for risk. The prevailing moods of the stock and bond markets are just two of the factors you must weigh in deploying your money. You should also make gradual adjustments in your mix of assets to correspond with your changing needs for capital growth, steady income or a combination of the two, particularly as you draw nearer to the day when you retire.

Key Questions to Answer Honestly

The perfect fund offers terrific long-term gains, bountiful dividends and never, ever loses money. Alas, such a paragon doesn't exist. No fund can deliver both high returns and safety. Investing always means weighing potential benefits against risks (see the box "The Five Faces of Risk That You Confront" on the next page). The cardinal rule is that the more safety you demand, the less return you can expect, and vice versa. That means you cannot search intelligently for the best funds without some soul searching first. These questions will help you define what's best for you.

Are you seeking growth, income or safety?

You're a growth investor if your key need is to build capital for a major future expense that's five or more years away, such as your kids' college education or your own retirement. The best funds for you invest mainly for capital appreciation. Such funds have a strong record of appreciation over long periods but are also the most prone to harsh short-term setbacks. As a result, you shouldn't consider yourself a growth investor unless you can endure painful stretches when your fund is down 20% or more. If you want your funds to help you pay ongoing expenses, such as your living costs in retirement, you're an income investor. Look at funds invested partly in bonds and sporting above-average yields. If you need money for an expense you will incur within a few years, what you need from your funds is safety. Your best choices are ultrasafe money-market funds. The drawback is that their yields have been achingly low in recent years.

Are you comfortable with risk? Think of risk as the entry fee you pay to invest. You can choose to take a lot or a little. But you can never avoid it entirely. The payback for assuming more risk is potential return. The most aggressive stock funds, for example, have suffered precipitous falls of 20% or so in their worst years. But their long-

The Five Faces of Risk That You Confront

Astute asset allocation begins with a careful analysis of your investments and other aspects of your financial life to see how each of these affects your exposure to the following types of risk.

▪ **Inflation risk.** Rising prices will reduce the purchasing power of an investment. An annual inflation rate of 5% over 15 years will cut the value of $1,000 to $480. Overcautious investors who hoard assets in money-market funds may not earn enough to outpace rising prices. Rising inflation also erodes the value of future income generated by investments with fixed payments, most notably long-term bonds.

▪ **Interest-rate risk.** Rising rates will cause investments to drop in price. Higher rates make yields on existing bonds less attractive, so their market values decline. Rising rates also hurt stocks by making their dividend yields less appealing. People who invest borrowed money through margin accounts or have other types of floating-rate debt increase their risk because higher interest rates cut into their net profits.

▪ **Economic risk.** Slower growth in the economy will cause investments to fall in price. Shares of small growth companies may shrink because they require a booming economy to sustain their robust earnings gains. Cyclical companies, such as automakers and chemical producers, can't easily cut their hefty fixed costs during a recession. So their earnings and share prices may well nosedive. Economic downturns can also undercut junk bonds issued by financially weak firms that might default.

▪ **Market risk.** This includes such factors as political developments and Wall Street fads that can batter investment markets. Tax law changes, trade agreements, program trading and the quirks of investor psychology all contribute to market risk, which has accounted for much of the stock market's day-to-day volatility. Gold also carries considerable market risk because its price moves sharply when political or military upheavals in other countries encourage the flight of capital.

▪ **Specific risk.** This covers occurrences that may affect only a particular company or industry. Poor management or bad luck can dampen earnings or even bankrupt a company. And high-flying growth stocks are particularly vulnerable to earnings disappointments. Individuals take on a high degree of specific risk when they buy stock in a firm with a heavy debt burden or invest in specialty stock funds, often called sector funds, that concentrate their holdings in a single field such as healthcare. Specific risk also includes the chance that government regulation will harm a particular group of companies.

term returns, which lately averaged close to 12% annually, make a compelling case for investing in them anyway. Stocks almost always beat bonds in the long run. This has been true for most of this century despite wars, economic crises and global change. Thus risk isn't necessarily bad as long as you don't take on more than you can handle.

How soon do you need the money? The longer you're planning to hold on to your fund shares, the more you can afford to shoot for the stock market's higher returns. Say you had invested in the S&P 500 index at the start of any calendar year in the past 55 years and pulled out after 12 months. According to the research firm Ibbotson Associates, you would have made money two out of three times. Had you held on for five years, your odds of making a profit would have improved to four out of five. And if you stood by your stocks for 10 years, you would have finished in the black 96% of the time.

How much could you bear to lose? No matter how impressive a fund's long-term record may be, you won't score big if you bail out when the fund turns temporarily cold. So ask yourself how much you could stand to see your investment plunge in a given year before pulling the ripcord. If you're willing to stomach losses of 10% or more in a year, you're an aggressive investor. That suits you for high-risk, high-return funds such as those invested for aggressive growth or in small-company stocks. A 5% threshold suggests you're interested in trading off some performance for safety in, say, total return funds that blend high-yielding stocks and bonds. If you're unwilling to tolerate any losses, you're too conservative for virtually any stock fund and all but the safest bond portfolios. Your options are money-market funds or those invested in government bonds of short or intermediate maturities.

Do you need lots of hand holding? Funds can be sold in either of two ways. Many funds are peddled by stockbrokers, independent planners and insurance agents. You get the salesperson's advice in choosing your fund. But the fund will deduct a commission (the load) from your investment either in an up-front fee of 4% to 8.5% or in some combination of redemption charges and ongoing annual charges. No-loads are sold by fund sponsors directly to investors without commission. The money usually changes hands by mail or by bank wire, though big outfits like Fidelity and Dreyfus have walk-in offices in many cities. Note, however, that not all no-loads are free of commissions. Many of Fidelity's directly sold funds carry so-called low loads of 2% to 3%, which the company itself pockets. The low load isn't as onerous as the charges levied by broker-sold funds. But you don't get any advice for your money either. Otherwise, there's no difference in performance between load and no-load funds. So whether to go load or no-load hinges on how much you value a salesperson's fund-picking prowess and advice.

Plumb Your Tolerance for Pain

To identify potential pitfalls in your fund strategy, fill out the worksheet "Evaluate Your Portfolio's Risk Level Now" beginning on page 68. Then you need to decide how to redeploy assets to reduce your exposure. Don't limit your inventory to investments that are kept in a brokerage account. Your earning power probably is by far your most valuable asset; equity in a home may come next. Many investors also have substantial assets invested in company pension plans or insurance policies with significant cash values. And entrepreneurs should take a close reading of the risks that threaten the value of their small business.

Risk can creep up on even vigilant fund investors. Your holdings in a retirement plan may grow more quickly than you realize, particularly if you make regular contributions or reinvest your returns. Growth in one asset can throw a portfolio out of balance if other investments don't keep up. If a prolonged bull market boosts the value of your stock funds, you may need to sell some shares to restore the balance between stocks and other assets. Similarly, when a single fund does extremely well, you have to consider whether it's time to shed some shares. Be especially wary of loading up on your company's stock through savings plans sponsored by your firm. If the company runs into trouble, both your job and your stock could be endangered at the same time. To gauge your own situation, you will need to conduct a survey of your investments and other aspects of your finances.

Stocks and stock funds. They are vulnerable to the possibility that skittish investors will panic for some reason and drive share prices down en masse (an example of market risk). But risks related to inflation, interest rates or economic growth may vary considerably. For example, a sharp increase in the inflation rate depresses stock prices because it may reduce the purchasing power of future dividends to shareholders. What's more, inflation generally coincides with higher interest rates, which draw investors from stocks to bonds. Because firms such as retailers, consumer product manufacturers and service companies can more readily pass along cost increases to customers, they have a better chance to prosper during periods of high inflation. Slowing economic growth hurts some firms more than others. Manufacturers with high overhead, known as cyclicals, cannot easily cut costs when a recession slices sales. So their earnings quickly tail off. Many small growth companies also require an expanding economy to sustain their earnings growth and stock prices. By contrast, firms that sell necessities such as food or clothing often shine even in a lackluster economy. Since overseas stocks are partly immune to changes in the American economy and markets, they may stand firm while U.S. stocks sink. Unlike domestic issues, however, foreign shares carry currency risk. A weaker dollar abroad helps

Evaluate Your Portfolio's Risk Level Now

Most people shield some of their fund investments against different types of risk. But few balance all of their assets so that they are well protected. This quiz can help you identify your points of vulnerability. With each question, you will accumulate points for one or more of the five major investment risks that are described in the main text. Write the points in the boxes below. Then total the points for each risk and interpret your scores as follows. Fewer than five points is low. Five to 10 points is moderate. Above 10 points is high. While you may want to vary your exposure to different categories of risk, depending on your personal circumstances and outlook for the financial markets, any score that comes in above 10 points should set off alarm bells.

Once you have identified vulnerabilities, you can take steps to shore up your defenses. Say that you score high for inflation risk and low for market risk. You might balance your portfolio better by switching some cash from money-market funds to those invested in stocks or gold-mining shares. While your risk of a temporary decline in the value of your portfolio will increase, you will have a better chance of outpacing inflation over the long term.

In answering the questions, don't make the mistake of overlooking funds located in 401(k) accounts, IRAs or any other savings or deferred-compensation plans. It may be difficult to pin down the value of some assets. For instance, you may have a universal life policy with an important investment component. Just make the best estimates that you can. It isn't necessary to be exact. But it is important that your inventory be as complete as possible.

Questions

Questions	INFLATION RISK	INTEREST-RATE RISK	ECONOMIC RISK	MARKET RISK	SPECIFIC RISK
Are your assets diversified among fewer than four of these five categories—stocks, real estate, gold, bonds and cash? If yes, score one point for each risk.					
Are more than 35% of your assets invested in any one of the five categories? If yes, score one point for each risk.					
Is at least 10% of your portfolio in assets such as gold, natural-resource stocks or high-grade collectibles such as rare stamps? If no, score one point for inflation risk.					
Is at least 30% of your portfolio in investments such as growth stocks and real estate, which are likely to produce long-term capital gains that can outpace inflation? If no, score two points for inflation risk.					
Are your real estate and gold investments held primarily in assets such as gold-mining shares and REITs (real estate investment trusts), which tend to fluctuate with the stock market? If yes, score one point for market risk.					
Do you generally keep at least 15% of your portfolio in cash equivalents such as Treasury bills or money-market funds? If no, score two points for interest-rate risk.					
Is more than 30% of your portfolio composed of assets such as long-term government bonds, CDs (certificates of deposit) or annuities that promise to pay investors fixed payments over a period of many years? If yes, then score three points each for inflation and interest-rate risk.					

	INFLATION RISK	INTEREST-RATE RISK	ECONOMIC RISK	MARKET RISK	SPECIFIC RISK
Do highly volatile zero-coupon bonds account for more than 30% of your fixed-income assets? If yes, score two points each for inflation and interest-rate risk.					
Do small growth stocks or junk bonds, which may fall sharply in a recession, account for more than 25% of your portfolio? If yes, score three points for economic risk.					
Do you switch money among different assets to try and catch the highs and lows of different investment markets? If yes, score two points for market risk.					
Do you use dollar cost averaging or a similar plan that involves adding money to your investment portfolio at regular intervals? If no, score two points for market risk.					
Is more than 20% of your portfolio concentrated in a single industry? If yes, score three points each for economic risk, market risk and specific risk.					
Do stocks or bonds issued by one company (including the one that you work for) or shares in a single mutual fund or limited partnership account for more than 15% of your assets? If yes, score three points each for economic risk, market risk and specific risk.					
Does your share in a privately held business account for more than 30% of your portfolio? If yes, score one point for economic risk and four points for specific risk.					
Does a rental property account for more than 30% of your portfolio? If yes, score one point for economic risk and three points for specific risk.					
Do foreign stocks and shares of domestic companies with significant overseas sales account for less than 10% of your portfolio? If yes, score one point for economic risk.					
Will you need access in the next three to five years to principal in volatile assets such as stocks or long-term bonds? If yes, score one point each for inflation, interest-rate, economic and market risk.					
Do you have variable-rate loans such as mortgages or credit-card revolving debt that recently has amounted to 30% or more of the market value of your portfolio? If yes, score four points for interest-rate risk.					
Is 20% or more of your portfolio financed by loans or invested in highly leveraged assets such as options? If yes, score one point each for interest-rate and market risk.					
TOTAL					

to inflate returns earned by American investors on overseas assets, while a stronger dollar deflates them.

Bonds and bond funds. Their prices fall when interest rates rise. But the extent of the drop depends on a bond's maturity and the amount of its coupon. Short-term bonds fall slightly when interest rates move upward, and a high coupon also offers some protection against climbing rates. At the opposite extreme, zero-coupon bonds fall sharply when rates head higher. A recession generally brings lower interest rates, which boost bond prices. But some issues react negatively to the threat of an economic slowdown. So-called junk bonds, in particular, may lose ground because investors fear that financially weak firms will default and fail to make payments of interest and principal to bondholders on time. U.S. Treasury and high-grade corporate bonds gain the most during hard times because income investors seek them out as safe havens.

Gold and gold funds. The price of gold can skyrocket when the inflation rate rises rapidly. Between 1968 and 1988, the consumer price index posted nine annual spurts of 6% or more. During those years, gold rewarded investors with gains averaging 34% annually. Gold-mining stocks and the funds that own them are more volatile than the metal itself. A miners' strike might boost the price of bullion but cut profits at mining companies. Other tangible assets present their own problems.

Real estate investments. Although they tend to keep pace with inflation over time, they present other hazards. If you own a rental property, you run the risk that you won't find a tenant. A real estate partnership that owns several properties in different regions can reduce such risks through diversification. But it may lose value if tax changes or a recession drive down property values across the country. Real estate investment trusts, called REITs, and the funds that own them, can fluctuate with the stock market as well as with property values.

Gun for Long-Term Growth

History suggests that stocks return about 2.7 times as much as do money-market funds and twice as much as bonds in the long term. But from one month or one year to the next you can lose serious money in the stock market. The possibility of short-term losses is a constant in today's skittish market. So a prudent investor will take some elementary precautions. For starters, don't consider investing in stock funds unless you're reasonably sure you won't need the money within five years. That's roughly the length of the typical economic cycle. If you were unlucky enough to put your money in at a market peak, you may need the full cycle to recover your losses and make a profit. If you suffer a 30% loss in your first year of investing, for example, it would take you almost four years at a 10% annual return to get even. The best way to avoid such unfortunate timing is to ease into your funds gradually by making equal payments over a matter of months or years, regardless of whether the stock market is rising or falling (see "Tactics That Reduce Your Exposure" later in this chapter).

More and more investors whose goal is growth are focusing on fund managers' investment styles for the simple reason that people differ on what makes a stock appealing. By training or temperament, managers gravitate toward stocks with certain traits. Some favor those of small companies (market values under $1 billion). Others like large blue-chip firms (over $2 billion). And still others prefer companies in the middle called mid-caps. Within those sizes, managers may seek either fast-growing firms or seeming bargains. Learning where your fund fits in is more than just pigeonholing. Academic studies show that style accounts for at least 75% of a typical growth fund's return.

Small vs. large companies. Each of these two approaches has its own investment logic and its own roster of successful practitioners. Small-cap or mid-cap managers specialize in those companies on the theory that young, entrepreneurial firms have the most explosive growth potential. The risk, however, is that small-stock funds are prone to unpredictable downturns that can swiftly wipe out 10% to 20% of their value. Other managers prefer the stocks of corporate giants. The argument for them is that they are Wall Street's best source of stable profits. The problem is that it's hard for even the shrewdest managers to uncover hidden opportunities among the most widely followed stocks.

Growth vs. value approach. After size, the main style distinction is between so-called growth and value investors. The former want to own the fastest growing, most successful companies (e.g., the Microsofts, Wal-Marts, Home Depots and their successors) capable of expanding their earnings a brisk 15% or better a year. The problem is that such premium companies usually trade at rich prices relative to their earnings. Thus their stocks can fall hard in the event that earnings fail to live up to investors' lofty expectations. Value managers are the stock market's equivalent of flea market browsers. They're looking for cast-aside stocks trading at prices that may not reflect the true value of their assets or future earnings.

How do you discern a manager's style? For size distinctions, simply call the fund sponsor and ask for the fund's median market capitalization, or the total market value of the fund's median stock. To tell whether the manager is a growth getter or value seeker, look at the fund's yield and price-earnings ratio (calculated by references like Morningstar). A value fund generally will have a higher than average yield and a lower than average PE ratio. A growth fund will be the opposite.

Which size or style is best? Research suggests that over the long haul, small-company stocks beat out big ones, and value stocks have the edge over growth. For example, Trinity Investment Management based in Cambridge, Mass. studied growth vs. value stocks over a recent 24-year stretch and found that value won, returning 12% annually relative to growth's 9%. Here's one rationale. Because value stocks by definition already trade at depressed prices, they tend to fall less far in bear markets. In the five losing markets included in the Trinity study, value stocks dropped an average of about 17%, while the typical growth stock lost 25%. As for small-caps, Trinity's calculations show that these stocks edged out large companies by nearly one percentage point a year (or 10.4% to 9.6%). Over shorter time spans, however, it's a much tighter race in which each of the different styles takes its turn in the lead for periods that generally last two to five years.

Trying to predict precisely when the cycle is going to shift is as futile as any other kind of market timing. That's why choosing among investment styles is primarily a tool of diversification. By owning stock funds of every style, you can effectively smooth out the inevitable ups and downs of Wall Street fashions. Just as important, you'll be able to distinguish between fund managers whose performance is lagging merely because their investment approach is currently out of vogue and those who simply have lost their touch.

Fatten Your Profits Overseas

Foreign stock funds are ideal if you lack the resolve to become fluent in faraway markets. There are four subcategories based upon breadth of investing focus. The broadest are global funds, which can invest anywhere in the world including the U.S., followed by international funds, which invest everywhere in the world except the U.S. Then there are regional funds, which invest in a specific segment of the globe such as Latin America, and single-country funds.

Investors first beginning to diversify worldwide can probably cut through the confusion of choices by ignoring global and single-country funds and zeroing in on internationals. Why? The problem with global funds is that the manager's freedom to acquire U.S. stocks can negate your whole purpose of buying the fund—to diversify overseas. The typical global fund today puts some 40% of its assets in the U.S. Thus if you're aiming to reallocate a portfolio mix to contain, say, one-quarter holdings abroad, you could calibrate that percentage more precisely with an international fund, a pure overseas play. And many small investors will find single-country funds too risky, narrowly focused or both.

Factor in political and currency risks. For many small investors, funds are often the only viable vehicles for venturing into uncharted international waters. Most foreign stock markets do not impose reporting standards on companies that are as stringent as those enforced by the SEC here. So such financial information is not only harder to obtain but also tends to be less reliable. Worse, buying foreign securities exposes you to two special types of risk. The first is political risk, or the danger that unexpected electoral shifts or governmental instability will adversely affect a market. For example, shares in the closed-end Mexico Fund tumbled following the assassination of the leading presidential candidate. The other worry that's commonly looming over foreign investing is currency risk, the danger that the lately anemic value of the U.S. dollar abroad will rebound and shrink your returns overseas.

Suppose, for example, you take $1,000 and convert it into Japanese yen at a time when the dollar is worth 100 yen. Then you spend those 100,000 yen on 100 shares of a Japanese stock fund at 1,000 yen per share. What would happen if the dollar rises in value to 125 yen but your fund goes nowhere? If you decided to bail out, you would get the same price you paid (100,000 yen) but net only $800 after converting your proceeds back into dollars (100,000 divided by 125). So you lost 20% (not counting brokerage commissions) on your investment even though your Japanese fund held firm. Of course, if the dollar fell the same percent against the yen, you would have profited 20% on that stagnant fund. The reassuring news is that the dollar's currency swings tend to cancel each other out over the long term, leaving no significant statistical impact on portfolio performance. But the short-term currency threat may rule out the notion of international diversification for some conservative investors.

Angle for Both Income and Growth

Reflect on the fact that 75% of bond fund investors don't spend a penny of the income that their funds produce. Instead, they reinvest their payout in more fund shares, suggesting many mistakenly use bond funds as tools for capital growth. Yet the bond market's historic return is only about half that of stocks. In other words, if you rely entirely on bonds to meet your long-range financial goals, you risk coming up short. What about bonds' reputation for lower risk? Well, it's generally true, but not always. As interest rates zigzagged through the 1980s, long-term corporate and government bonds were nearly 20% more volatile than was the S&P 500 index. Then you have to factor in the pernicious effect of inflation. Looking back at all the five-year periods since 1937, the stocks in the S&P 500 beat inflation by an average of 7.3 percentage points a year. But intermediate-term Treasury bonds (those maturing in five to 10 years) nosed out rising prices by just one point.

A catchall called total return funds. If you have financial goals more than five years off, take a deep breath and admit that at least some of your money belongs in stocks. That doesn't mean you have to dive into the deep end of the market where the aggressive growth funds swim, however. Instead, wade into total return funds, a moderate-risk category embracing such major subsets as equity income and balanced portfolios. Some seek capital gains as a secondary goal by supplementing their bond holdings with high-dividend stocks or convertible securities. Convertibles are essentially hybrids (issued either as bonds or preferred stock) that pay fixed income the same way that bonds do but can be exchanged for shares of the issuing company's common stock at a specified price. Total return funds aim to blend the bondlike attributes of steady income with stocklike spurts of capital appreciation. That has allowed them to grow several percentage points a year faster than bond funds while avoiding the unnerving volatility of racier stock funds.

Total return funds that go 40% or more into fixed-income securities are about a third less volatile than those that traditionally keep 85% or more of their portfolios in stocks. Such stock-heavy total return funds are about 25% less topsy-turvy than pure growth funds. A total return fund's subcategory can give a quick insight as to where it fits on the continuum of stocks vs. bonds. Flexible-income funds, for example, rely most heavily on bonds, typically holding just 20% of their assets in stocks. Convertible securities funds store at least 60% of their money in bonds or other fixed-income choices that can be traded in for shares of common stock. The trade-off? Convertibles typically yield one to three percentage points less than straight corporate bonds while offering at least half the potential capital appreciation of the issuer's common stock. Balanced funds aim for a roughly 60-40 split between stocks and bonds, compared with about 75-25 for equity income portfolios. By comparison, so-called growth and income funds tend to be at least 80% invested in stocks.

If you're considering total return funds that keep more than 20% of their assets in bonds, call the fund and request figures on its bonds' *average weighted maturity* and *credit quality.* As explained later in this chapter, short-term and intermediate issues hold their value far better than long-term bonds with maturities of 10 years or more when interest rates rise. Credit quality is a concern on securities rated below investment grade (BB or lower from Standard & Poor's or Baa or lower from Moody's). The greater the proportion of suspect IOUs, the more susceptible the fund is to losses when the economy slows and issuers struggle to pay interest.

Lock in Reliable Dividends

Income-minded investors love bond funds that yield regular, generous dividends. Such funds are particularly attractive to retirees and other people who depend on investment earnings for a large portion of their everyday living expenses. Many growth-oriented investors also own the funds to help diversify their holdings and lower the risk inherent in fairly aggressive stock portfolios. Bonds obligate the issuing company or government to pay interest, usually at regular intervals, and to repay the face value of the bond at maturity. A large number of these funds provide tax-exempt income by investing exclusively in municipal bonds issued by city and state governments.

Why total return matters most. Unlike a bank certificate of deposit, a bond fund's yield isn't guaranteed. Your total return depends not only on the dividends you get but also on the price you receive when you sell your fund shares. The value of bonds (and the funds that own them) appreciates when interest rates decline and falls when interest rates increase. Generally speaking, the higher a bond fund's yield, the greater the overall credit risk, maturity and volatility of the bonds the fund holds.

There is no credit risk, or likelihood of a bond's issuer defaulting on its interest or principal payments, among funds that invest solely in bonds or mortgage-backed securities guaranteed by the federal government. Nor should there be any fears over the safety of funds whose bond holdings have the highest credit ratings from Standard & Poor's or Moody's, which grade companies and municipalities from AAA (tops) to D (in default). Financially solid issuers pay the least to borrow money, so you get lower yields. To grab higher income, however, some funds concentrate on lower quality issues, commonly called junk bonds, that are rated less than investment grade (B or below). While remarkably few junk bonds have defaulted over time, they are the ones investors dump first when business conditions sour or bond prices slump across the board, causing their prices to drop the most.

How to place your bond bets. Long-term bonds (maturing in more than 10 years) almost always yield more than intermediate issues (five to 10 years) or short-term ones (five years or fewer) because their prices are the most sensitive to fluctuations in interest rates. If rates were to rise by just one percentage point, the price of recently issued 20-year Treasury bonds would fall about 9%. Three-year Treasury notes would drop only 2% to 3%. So if you think interest rates are going to rise substantially, you should only consider funds that limit their holdings to bonds of short or inter-mediate terms. If you expect rates to fall, as MONEY has forecast, you would definitely favor long-term bond funds. Each fund generally keeps its holdings' maturities within a range specified in the prospectus. To find out a fund's average maturity, you must call the fund.

Many advisers suggest that you build your portfolio of bond funds around a conservative core of short and intermediate taxable funds. The rationale? Five-year Treasuries lately have yielded 93% as much as a 30-year Treasury with less than 50% of the interest-rate risk. As your bond portfolio grows, you can add funds of different maturities or credit quality, depending on your outlook for interest rates and tolerance of risk. Here's a rundown of your fund choices.

■ **U.S. Governments.** These funds invest in bonds issued by the U.S. Treasury or federal government agencies. The safety from default is all but absolute, which makes government funds tops for conservative income seekers. The trade-off is lower yields. Vanguard Fixed-Income Long-Term U.S. Treasury, for example, recently paid slightly less than Vanguard Fixed-Income Long-Term Corporate, a corporate fund of the same average maturity. Note, however, that in Treasury-only bond funds, the lower yield is at least partly made up by the fact that the dividends usually escape state taxes. Be aware too that government backing does not protect you against interest-rate risk. A Treasury portfolio will drop in price when interest rates rise.

■ **Mortgage-backed securities.** One species of government fund specializes in these issues, which represent shares in investment pools consisting of home mortgages. They're backed by federal agencies with such cute nicknames as Ginnie Mae (the Government National Mortgage Association) and Freddie Mac (the Federal Home Loan Mortgage Corporation). They offer yields 0.5 to 1.5 percentage points higher than those on Treasury funds. The higher yields are partly a trade-off for prepayment risk, one peculiar to mortgage-backed securities. When interest rates fall, homeowners rush to refinance their mortgages at lower rates. As the old pooled mortgages are paid off, funds holding the securities are, in effect, handed back parts of their principal, which they then must reinvest at lower prevailing yields. Thus mortgage funds get a far smaller boost than Treasuries from falling rates.

■ **Corporates.** Such bond funds allow you to invest in businesses ranging from America's most solid to its shakiest. Entries in our high-grade corporate category hold bonds carrying an average credit rating only a step below governments, making them an appealing alternative for investors who want to earn more than government funds pay but who don't want to get swamped by credit risk. At the other end of the credit spectrum are high-yield corporates, better known as junk bond funds. They focus on the bonds of debt-burdened behemoths and unproven start-ups. Unlike other bond funds, junkers are at their best in a strengthening economy because a healthy business climate reduces the risk of defaults. Indeed, during the recent economic recovery, junk bond funds have been one of the hottest fixed-income categories. Lately, however, the yield spread between Treasuries and junk funds has been at the low end of their range. So high-yield issues don't have as much room to recreate the glory days of recent years.

■ **Tax-exempt municipals.** These funds buy bonds issued by cities, states and other local government entities. Also known as municipal bond funds, all of them produce dividends free of federal income tax. The dividends from so-called single-state muni funds, which invest entirely within the borders of one state, are exempt from state and local taxes as well for resident shareholders. Muni funds are most appealing to people in the 28% federal tax bracket and above. Analysts say that a growing appetite for tax-frees and a shrinking supply also bodes well for muni prices. One reason is that aging baby boomers will increasingly need to save on a tax-sheltered basis. But you still need to be cautious. Unless otherwise stated in the prospectus, most muni funds tend to hold longer-term securities than comparable corporate or government funds, making the muni funds more sensitive to interest-rate fluctuations. Also check the fund's annual report to make sure that it isn't trying to pump up yield by loading up on the offerings of frequently shaky muni issuers like industrial development agencies or hospitals. Analysts say that the slight increase in yield just isn't worth the considerably greater default risk.

Foreign bonds. Diversification is the main reason to invest a portion of your fixed-income portfolio overseas. As in stocks, international diversification in bonds can reduce risk and enhance long-term gains. That's because the U.S. and foreign bond markets rarely move in unison. When one is down, the other is often rising. Remember, however, that foreign bond funds face the same currency risks discussed earlier. When you invest in foreign securities of any kind you run the risk that a rising dollar will shrink their value. Most international bond funds try to minimize such risks by using hedging techniques in the foreign exchange markets. Hedging can be expensive, shaving your fund's profits by as much as 5%. And fund managers can guess wrong about shifts in exchange rates. Thus investors with long time frames generally are better off buying foreign bond funds with a policy of riding out currency swings, which experts say tend to equalize over periods of five to 10 years.

The Ideal Blend for Life's Phases

Why does asset allocation determine such a large portion of an investor's return? According to researchers, the basic reason is that different types of investments don't rise and fall at the same time. By diversifying among stocks, bonds or cash, you can usually offset losses in one asset category with gains in another. For example, in October 1987, when stocks plummeted nearly 22%, long-term bonds rose 6%. The opposite proved true in 1994. Bonds tumbled 3%, while the S&P 500 eked out a 1% gain. While diversification can't guarantee that you'll never lose money, it can reduce your portfolio's overall risk and dramatically improve your odds of reaching your investment goals.

To determine the most efficient mix of investments, experts first look at the correlation between various asset classes. Correlation is the technical term for comparing how different assets perform relative to one another over varying market cycles. The analysts measure correlation on a scale of 1.0 (two assets move precisely in tandem over time) to -1.0 (the investments always move in opposite directions). You ideally want to build a portfolio of different types of assets that are not closely correlated to one another. That way, you won't get clobbered by all your investments dropping in value at roughly the same time.

What's more, a properly diversified portfolio lets you put some of your money in potentially high-paying assets that otherwise might be too risky. You perform this alchemy by combining them with investments to which the high fliers are only weakly correlated. For example, a portfolio entirely invested in the large-company stocks that make up the S&P 500 would have gained over 14% a year during the past two decades. But you could have earned 16% a year over the same time with a portfolio invested 65% in S&P 500 stocks, 20% in overseas stocks (with a 0.5 correlation to U.S. blue chips) and 15% in small-company shares (a 0.8 correlation to the S&P 500). In allocating assets, the pros rely not only on stocks' and bonds' past performance but also on estimates of their potential future returns. These predictions are based on forecasts of how market cycles will affect the performance of different asset classes. The model portfolios in this chapter are based on projections that over the next 10 years or so large-company stocks will climb an average of 12% annually, bonds will rise 5% a year and cash investments such as Treasury bills will edge up almost 4% annually.

Profiting through life's passages. As you grow older, start a family and move closer to retirement, your investment goals and taste for risk change. Your fund portfolio should change along with you. Younger people, for example, can afford to aim for high returns with aggressive stock funds because they have many years to recover from market slumps. But as you get closer to retirement, you need to shift to a more cautious allocation that will preserve your gains. There's a second, equally powerful argument in favor of asset allocation. Academic studies show that about 90% of investors' returns come from the right combination of assets, with the remainder derived from their skill in picking securities and from timely trading. To help you design your own allocation, MONEY surveyed many experts to devise a model fund portfolio for each of the four major stages in most people's working lives—starting out, raising a family, peak earning years and retirement living (our depictions of the portfolios begin at right).

Aiming high in your 20s to early 30s. You now have about 30 years before early retirement. So you can afford to gun for growth by stashing at least 75% of your portfolio in stock funds. Go for as much as 100% if you feel comfortable riding out market swings. Those who tend to get queasy in roller-coaster markets might put as much as 25% of their money in bond funds, which pay interest that will help stabilize most portfolios. Based on past performance, this 75-25 lineup has the potential to return over 9% annually.

Getting Started in Your 20s to Early 30s

Single person, late twenties, with $10,000 saved

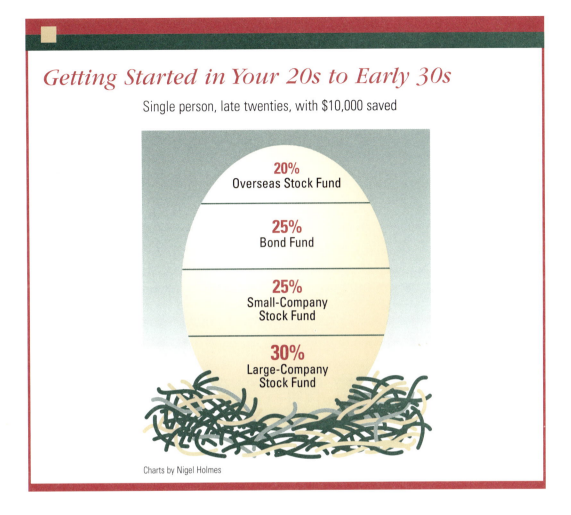

20%
Overseas Stock Fund

25%
Bond Fund

25%
Small-Company
Stock Fund

30%
Large-Company
Stock Fund

Charts by Nigel Holmes

For beginners with small savings, a single fund that buys large-company stocks is a sound choice. Blue chips tend to offer solid capital appreciation with less volatility than smaller stocks. Nervous investors might want to opt for a balanced or asset-allocation fund instead. These all-in-one portfolios typically keep about 60% of their assets in stocks and the rest in risk-cushioning bonds and other fixed-income investments. Investors who have $10,000 or more ought to assemble a diversified portfolio of funds. Allocate about 30% of your assets to large-company stocks, 25% to small-company stocks (those with annual revenues of $1 billion or less) and 20% to overseas stocks. Small stocks historically have outpaced their bigger brothers, though with greater volatility. Overseas stocks can spice up your portfolio because many foreign economies, particularly developing ones in Asia and Latin America, are likely to grow much faster than ours over the next decade. The risks you face are political instability and adverse swings in the value of the dollar.

For a smoother ride to those higher returns, you might include both value and growth-stock funds in your portfolio. Value managers look for out-of-favor companies with share prices that do not fully reflect their earnings prospects or asset values. By contrast, growth-stock managers, as the name suggests, prefer companies with rapidly accelerating revenues and earnings, even though their shares typically will command premium prices. You can't really predict which investing style will be more successful in any given year. Studies show that over periods of 20 years or more, however, value has a slight performance advantage over growth.

As for your fixed-income holdings, put about 15% of your money in investment-grade bonds with intermediate maturities of five to 10 years. Studies show that five-year issues produce roughly 95% of the return of 30-year issues with only half the volatility. About 5% of your money should go into a convertible bond fund, which will give you a shot at capital gains, or to a high-yield fund, which takes on extra risk in pursuit of the fatter yields paid by junk bonds. But steer clear of bond funds that carry sales charges or fees that total more than 1% of net assets. Their managers generally can't overcome these high expenses with superior performance. (Fees are listed in a fund's prospectus.)

Family planning in your early 30s to 40s. With young families to provide for and mortgages to pay off, many investors in this age group prefer to reduce their portfolios' risk level. Just don't overdo it. You will be working for another 20 years or more, so you should keep at least 75% of your money in stocks. You can achieve that balance by gradually trimming back your stock funds and moving the excess cash to a money-mar-

Raising a Family in Your Early 30s to 40s

Couple, thirties, two preschoolers, $50,000 saved

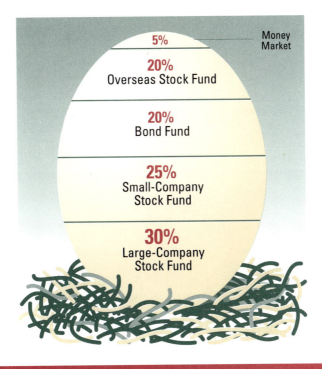

- 5% — Money Market
- 20% Overseas Stock Fund
- 20% Bond Fund
- 25% Small-Company Stock Fund
- 30% Large-Company Stock Fund

ket fund. Overall, our model is designed to give you average returns of about 8.75% annually. At this stage, you should further diversify your bond holdings. High earners should consider transferring the money in their convertible or high-yield corporate bond fund to a tax-free municipal bond fund and adding enough money so that it becomes 10% of the portfolio. A taxable alternative is an international bond fund. Fixed-income markets in the U.S. and abroad generally move in different directions. So you will offset a falling market with one that is on the rise. Foreign bond funds, of course, can respond sharply to currency fluctuations. But if you can let your money ride for at least 10 years, the swings will likely even out.

Investing in Your Prime 40s to 50s

Couple, early fifties, three teens, $200,000 saved

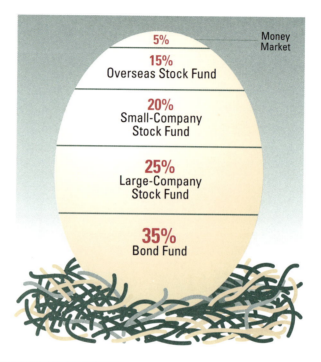

5%
Money Market

15%
Overseas Stock Fund

20%
Small-Company Stock Fund

25%
Large-Company Stock Fund

35%
Bond Fund

Hitting stride in your early 40s to 50s. You have reached your peak earning years—just in time to pay your kids' college bills. Don't let that serve as an excuse to neglect your savings. Stocks should still be the centerpiece of your portfolio. But ease back on risk by reducing your exposure to large-company stocks to 25%, small caps to about 20% and overseas stocks to 15%. This model aims to provide you with average total returns of around 8% annually. You can add greater stability to your portfolio by emphasizing value funds. Since value funds focus on bargain-priced companies, they tend to fall less far than their high-flying growth peers during market corrections. And the stocks in value funds tend to pay divi-

Nearing Retirement in Your Early 50s to 60s

Couple, mid sixties, empty nesters, $400,000 saved

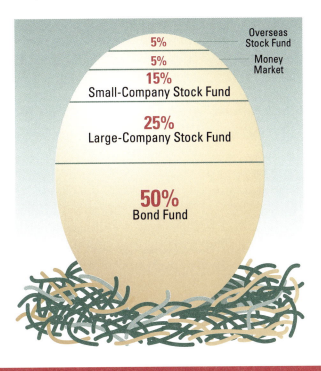

Overseas Stock Fund — 5%

Money Market — 5%

15% Small-Company Stock Fund

25% Large-Company Stock Fund

50% Bond Fund

dends that will bolster your returns in down years. In the fixed-income portion of your portfolio, you might seek additional security by cutting international bonds to 5% and exchanging your intermediate-term corporate bond fund for one that holds government issues. Investors in the 28% bracket or above, however, will probably do better with tax-exempt bonds. To earn high returns with minimum risk, look for muni funds with annual fees of less than 1% that hold mainly bonds rated A or higher.

Kicking back in your early 50s to 60s. With retirement around the corner, you may be tempted to cash in your stock funds and tuck the proceeds into principal-preserving bond or money-market funds. That could prove to be a bad move. At 50 you still have a lifetime of at least 30 years ahead of you. If inflation stays at 3% a year, that will cut the purchasing power of today's dollar in half in only 12 years. Thus you should still hold a roughly 45% stake in stocks. Such a model portfolio should produce average returns of around 7.5% a year. In addition, now is an excellent time to move out of international bonds entirely and into U.S. Government issues for greater safety. Truly risk-averse investors might anchor their portfolios with Treasury notes, which come due in two to 10 years, because their principal at maturity and interest payments are federally guaranteed.

Tactics That Reduce Your Exposure

Once you decide how to allocate the money in your portfolio, try to resist the urge to invest it all at once. Instead, divide the money into equal dollar amounts and move it into your chosen funds once a month or once a quarter over a year or two. Such periodic investing, commonly called dollar cost averaging, forces you to buy more fund shares when the prices are low and fewer when they are high. Another advantage is that it keeps you from yielding to panic in a market downturn. Variations of this technique will let you take full advantage of price dips, prevent you from getting badly hurt by sudden spikes and help assure that you reach your financial goals. Here are four strategies that rely mainly on stock funds.

Dollar cost averaging simplified. With this most basic form of periodic investing, you put a set amount each month (say, $200) in a stock fund. When stock prices fall, your $200 buys more fund shares. When prices rise, your money buys fewer. That way, you keep your fund shares' average cost relatively low as shown in the table "Comparing Tactics for Cutting Risk" at right. If you had invested $200 a month some 10 years ago in

Comparing Tactics for Cutting Risk

If you had used the value averaging method over the past 10 years, you would have earned returns averaging 15% annually, far more than with any of the other risk-cutting strategies shown below and explained in this chapter. In today's skittish market, however, investing experts say the three other techniques may carry less risk. In our table, we assumed that a hypothetical investor had an account with the Vanguard Index 500 Fund, which closely mimics the S&P 500 index. In the case of two related strategies, constant ratio planning and variable installment, we linked the Index 500 Fund with the Vanguard Money Market Reserves Prime Fund.

STRATEGY	MONTHLY CONTRIBUTION	TOTAL AMT. INVESTED	PORTFOLIO VALUE	AVERAGE ANNUAL RETURN	AVG. COST PER SHARE
Value averaging	Varies	$23,540	$49,400	15.1%	$20.90
Dollar cost averaging	$200	24,000	49,400	13.8	21.30
Constant ratio planning	200	24,000	40,400	9.9	28.00
Variable installment	200	24,000	40,300	9.9	29.30

Vanguard Index 500 Fund, which mimics the S&P 500 index, your $24,000 would have more than doubled to approximately $49,400. You can also try to boost your profits with a more advanced version, called progressive dollar cost averaging. This strategy takes into account inflation, the chief drawback of investing the same amount every month for years. With progressive averaging, you can increase your monthly contribution every year, or even every six months, by a set percentage. How much? Experts often recommend a manageable 10%. That will keep you far ahead of inflation as well as supercharge your savings. So an investor who starts out contributing $200 a month might step that up to $220 a year later on. If you had used this technique over the past 10 years, your $37,950 investment in the Vanguard Index 500 Fund would have grown to $69,800.

A wrinkle called value averaging.
Think of this as dollar cost averaging with attitude. Rather than investing a set monthly amount, you put in whatever is necessary to hit your goal. Let's say that you need $9,000 in three years for a down payment on a house. You first open a fund account with, perhaps, $200. Next, with the help of a financial calculator or compound interest tables found in your local library's reference section, you determine that your account's value must increase $200 a month to reach your target. The actual amount you invest each month will change as stock prices fluctuate. If the market is flat during the month you open your fund account, you simply invest an additional $200 in the second month, bringing your account's value to $400. If your fund's value falls by 12.5% during the second month, your account will dip to $350. Your third investment must then be $250, since your game plan calls for your account to be worth $600 in month three. If, however, stocks rise in the second month and boost your balance to $470, your third contribution must be only $130. What happens if the value of your holdings rises so rapidly that your account's value exceeds your monthly target? Value averaging calls for you to sell some shares. If your account increased to $700 in the third month, you would dump $100 of your holdings. Your profit would be taxable if you were investing outside of a tax-deferred account. Therefore, you might prefer a modified strategy called no-sell value averaging. When your portfolio value exceeds the target, you simply do nothing that month.

Value averaging beats dollar cost averaging most of the time. To accumulate $49,400 in the index fund using our example, you would have had to invest $24,000 10 years ago if you used dollar cost averaging but $23,540 with value averaging. That $460 saving may seem slim. Still, your money would have worked more efficiently, delivering both higher returns and a lower average cost per share.

Why Six Stock Funds Are Probably Plenty

How many stock funds should most investors strive to own? With the fund industry constantly cultivating scores of tempting new offerings, you may feel like filling your basket with one or two of each kind. According to a recent academic study, however, six funds are really all you need when it comes to investing in U.S. stocks.

Professors Walt Taylor of the University of Southern Mississippi and Jim Yoder of West Georgia College studied the performance of 168 U.S. stock funds over the period from 1978 through 1989. They found, not unexpectedly, that the risk to an investor's overall fund portfolio declined substantially as more and more funds were added to it. For the study, the authors defined risk in terms of standard deviation, which measures the degree that a portfolio's returns vary from one month to the next.

Cut risk 75% with just four funds. More surprising was the fact that most of the risk reduction (about 75%) occurred with just four funds. Because the study used a random sample, the results did not depend on which funds were chosen. After eight funds, there was very little further lessening of risk. And after 15 funds, there was almost none. Translating their statistical work into practical advice for investors, the professors believe the most effective way to achieve risk-reducing diversification is by mixing growth and value funds among your holdings. Growth funds favor companies posting rapidly rising earnings, while value funds hold stocks of companies thought to be selling for less than their intrinsic worth. They also believe in choosing funds that target stocks of different capitalizations, or total market values. Thus their recommended portfolio would consist of six funds—one growth and one value fund specializing in small, medium-size and large companies.

Role playing with your portfolio. John Markese, president of the American Association of Individual Investors, agrees with the idea of building a portfolio of role-playing funds. "In order to be diversified, investors need to have exposure to at least four managers who are experts in different segments of the market rather than the overall market," he says. Craig Litman, co-editor of investment newsletter *No-Load Fund Analyst*, suggests that investors put the finishing touches on their portfolios by adding an international stock fund. Says Litman: "Certainly, it wouldn't be unreasonable to utilize six to 10 funds for a well-rounded portfolio if you want to diversify across investment styles, across market capitalizations and across markets."

Check out constant ratio planning. This fairly conservative method calls for you to balance a stock fund investment against a less aggressive one, usually a money-market fund. You first decide how much risk you can take, then allocate your monthly investment between the two funds accordingly. Let's say you decide to split a $200 monthly investment evenly between a stock fund and a money fund. If stock prices rise, you eventually will have to shift money from your stock fund to your money fund to restore your fifty-fifty ratio. Investing experts recommend that you rebalance your portfolio whenever the ratio gets five percentage points out of whack. When stocks are rising, the more risk you're willing to take when you set the ratio, the more money you will make. In our example, a $200 monthly investment divided equally between the Vanguard Index 500 Fund and Vanguard Money Market would have grown to $40,400, about $9,000 less than with straight dollar averaging. But you would cut your risk roughly in half by stashing 50% of your cash in a money fund.

The appeal of variable installment. Like constant ratio, you start out by dividing your monthly investment equally between the funds. Then, when one fund lags the other, you direct your entire contribution to it. That way, you buy more shares when they are cheap and avoid putting money in investment categories that may be temporarily overvalued. Let's again assume you decide to invest $200 a month in a stock and a money fund. You start out by putting $100 into each. Whenever the stock fund's share price drops by an amount (let's say, 5%) that you have determined in advance, you put all of your next monthly investment into that fund. If its price rises 5%, you invest all your next monthly installment in the money fund. If you had invested a total of $24,000 10 years ago using this 5% variable installment method, your portfolio would have grown to around $40,300. Like constant ratio, variable installment would have earned you about $9,000 less than straight dollar cost averaging but would have carried less risk.

4

Make Hay With Your 401(k) Funds

*A*s one of the surviving toilers in today's downsized corporate work force, you probably don't give much thought to your 401(k) retirement plan. Sure, you get occasional 401(k) memos from your benefits department. But you don't have time to read them. You think there are maybe four or five choices of funds. But you don't really know what they are, or how they're doing. You can't really even remember which funds you own. You've got other things to worry about.

Think again. Managed properly, the funds in your 401(k) could make you a millionaire thanks to the plan's instant tax savings on the money you set aside, tax-deferred growth and the matching contributions most employers offer. Say you are a 25-year-old earning $30,000 a year. Now check out the graph "The Allure of Time Plus Tax Deferral" at right. If you stash 10% of your salary into your 401(k), you would end up with at least $1.3 million by age 65 if the funds in your plan earn annual returns averaging 6%. If you manage your funds wisely enough to boost that to 10%, your eventual take would top $3 million.

If that's not enough to get your attention, consider that 401(k)s aren't just your best shot at a comfortable retirement. They may be your only shot. Fewer and fewer companies are now funding traditional pension plans because they're just too expensive. Social Security faces well-known financing problems. Many experts say benefits will almost certainly be cut back or delayed

AGE 25   30

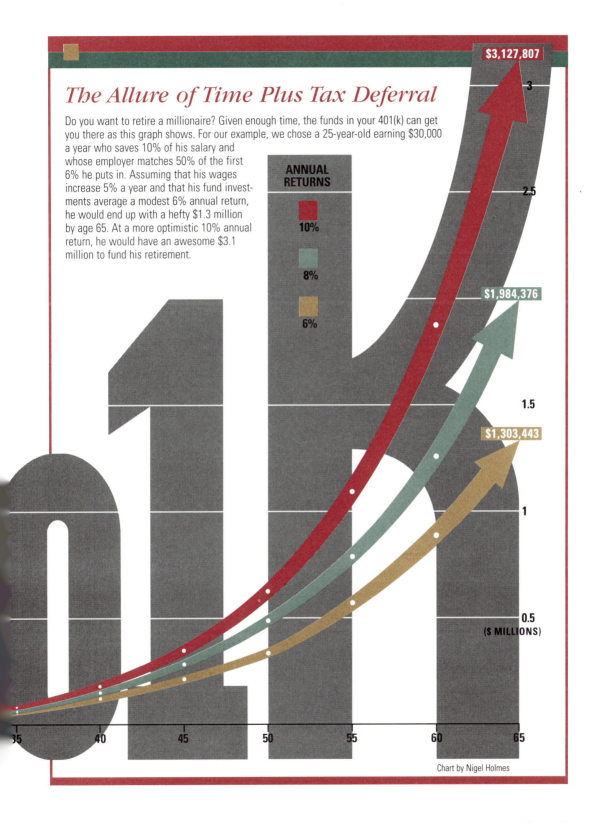

The Allure of Time Plus Tax Deferral

Do you want to retire a millionaire? Given enough time, the funds in your 401(k) can get you there as this graph shows. For our example, we chose a 25-year-old earning $30,000 a year who saves 10% of his salary and whose employer matches 50% of the first 6% he puts in. Assuming that his wages increase 5% a year and that his fund investments average a modest 6% annual return, he would end up with a hefty $1.3 million by age 65. At a more optimistic 10% annual return, he would have an awesome $3.1 million to fund his retirement.

ANNUAL RETURNS

- 10%
- 8%
- 6%

$3,127,807

$1,984,376

$1,303,443

3

2.5

1.5

1

0.5
($ MILLIONS)

35   40   45   50   55   60   65

Chart by Nigel Holmes

before the first wave of baby boomers begins to retire around the year 2010. "For many employees, 401(k) accounts will be their biggest single asset in retirement," says Bob Wuelfing of Access Research, an employee-benefits consultant based in Windsor, Conn. Indeed, the typical 401(k) account now holds nearly $40,000, and 10% boast $100,000 or more. With money pouring in at a rate of $1 billion a week, total 401(k) assets have reached $675 billion. By the year 2001, that number is expected to reach a staggering $1.5 trillion.

Of course, there's a catch to 401(k)s. It's totally up to you to make them work. You have to pony up the savings dollars, and you must make all the investment decisions. Save too little or pick the wrong investments, and your retirement may be considerably less comfortable. That's where this chapter will help. Your first step is to get acquainted with your 401(k), whose name comes from the section of the tax code that authorized it.

■ *Master the Basics of Your Plan*

If you aren't now eligible to join a 401(k) plan, you probably will be soon. Fully 95% of companies with more than 5,000 employees offer them. By 2001 nearly 30 million workers at some 340,000 companies will be able to join one, according to estimates by Access Research. If you work for a nonprofit group or in the public sector, you probably have access to similar retirement plans discussed in the box "Kissing Cousins to the 401(k)" on the right.

Three factors combine to make 401(k)s an unbeatable investment. Each dollar you tuck into your account is deducted from your taxable income. So you avoid federal and state taxes (except in Pennsylvania) on that money until you withdraw it. Someone in the 28% federal tax bracket who puts $2,400 into a 401(k) each year saves a quick $672 in federal taxes. What's more, all the interest, dividends and capital gains that you earn in your account continue to grow tax-free (again, until

Kissing Cousins to the 401(k)

If you work in the nonprofit or public sector, you may be offered your own tax-deferred savings program that sounds like a 401(k). But there are some important differences that you should know about.

■ **The lowdown on 403(b) plans.** These are offered to most workers at public schools, universities, nonprofit hospitals and similar organizations. They offer the same tax breaks as 401(k)s, but employer matching is much less common. In addition, many 403(b) investment offerings are annuities, which tend to have higher expenses than funds and, often, worse returns. More and more plans have been adding funds to their investment rosters, however. And it may make sense to switch even if you have to pay surrender charges on the annuity. Take the case of Bob Gomez, risk manager for Arizona State University. He moved from a poorly performing annuity to Fidelity Magellan in 1994. "It cost me $400 in surrender charges," says Gomez. "But I've earned nearly $2,000 in Magellan, so I'm way ahead." Also be aware that the IRS's 403(b) rules are extremely complex, and many nonprofits have inadvertently permitted their employees to put in too much money. The IRS lately has been forcing employers to bring their plans into compliance. The agency has not yet penalized any individuals as part of the crackdown. To be safe, ask your benefits officer to check that your contribution meets the guidelines.

■ **A wrinkle called 457 plans.** If you work for a state or local government, you probably have one of these. The plan lets you salt away up to $7,500 with the benefit of tax deferral but no employer match. The big difference between these plans and their cousins is that 457s do not hold your savings in trust. The money you set aside in a 457 is considered deferred compensation, so it belongs to your employer until you retire. That means your savings are at risk if your employer goes bankrupt. Such collapses are extremely rare, however. So the tax advantages of 457 plans make them too good to pass up.

withdrawal). And for good measure, nine out of 10 companies that offer 401(k)s sweeten the pot with money of their own. The corporate treasury typically will add 50¢ to every dollar you put in (capping its contribution at 3%

of your salary). Some large companies offer a dollar-for-dollar match. A few generous firms give even more.

Nearly 80% of workers who are eligible for 401(k)s participate in them. If you're among the balky 20% who don't, perhaps you think you can do better investing on your own outside the plan. But you are overlooking the awesome advantage of deferring taxes. Say a 35-year-old saves 6% of a $60,000 salary in a taxable portfolio of funds. If that money earns 8% a year, he would have roughly $284,000 by age 65, assuming a 28% federal tax rate. If he were to invest that money in a 401(k), he would end up with $571,700—more than twice as much. Of course, he would have to pay regular income taxes on the money he withdraws. But he would be able to take the money out gradually, lessening the tax bite, and leave the rest to continue growing tax deferred. Even if he rashly withdrew it all at once, he would be left with $366,000 after taxes. That's 29% more than he would have accumulated in a taxable investment.

Don't worry about tying up your cash. You may be wary of joining a 401(k) because you're reluctant to lock up your money for such a long time. But bear in mind that it's never completely off limits. True, short of becoming disabled, you generally can't get your money back before age 59.5 without owing a 10% penalty on the amount you withdraw plus regular income taxes. Most companies, however, let you borrow against your account without penalty or tax as long as you pay the loan back. Most also let you permanently withdraw money for so-called hardship expenses, though you will still face taxes and the 10% penalty. (For advice, see "Tap a 401(k) While You're Working" later in this chapter.) Moreover, if you leave the company, you can take your money with you, rolling it over into an IRA or possibly your new company's plan. That way you avoid paying penalties and taxes. Depending on how long you've been in the plan, you'll be able to take some or all of your company's matching contributions as well. In a process known as vesting, you are entitled to a greater

She's Starting Young and Saving Hard

At the age of 30, Kathryn Scott is determined not to get a late start on saving for retirement. "I went back to school at 27," she explains. While studying photojournalism at Western Kentucky University in Bowling Green, Scott couldn't exactly sock any money into an IRA account. But the bachelor's degree she picked up there helped her land a dream job in 1994, photographing news and sports events for Portland's daily paper, the *Oregonian.* "It feels great to be making money finally," she says of her $35,000 salary.

Last October, the instant she became eligible, she began putting 5% of her salary into the newspaper's 401(k) plan. "That was all I could manage," she says. "But I know I need to be as aggressive about investing as I possibly can." Last April, Scott doubled her contribution to 10% of pay. (The *Oregonian*'s 401(k) has a 15% maximum.)

At MONEY's request, financial planners Michael Chasnoff of Advanced Capital Strategies in Cincinnati and Alan Cohn of Sage Financial Group in Bala Cynwyd, Pa., reviewed Scott's 401(k) strategy as well as those of the families profiled later in this chapter. The pros say that Scott's goals are well within reach. "Assuming she puts 10% of her income in her 401(k) throughout her career and her investments earn a conservative 8.5%," says Chasnoff, "she should be independent by age 60 even without a penny of Social Security benefits." Though Scott still owes $10,000 on a student loan at 8% (payments run $250 a month), Chasnoff advises her not to pay it off early and shortchange her 401(k). "She'll make more in the long run by allowing as much money as possible to compound in her 401(k)," he says.

As for her investment selections, Chasnoff and Cohn say Scott has the right instincts. In May, her company replaced its former 401(k) asset manager with fund company T. Rowe Price. Scott transferred her money to one of the most aggressive of the plan's six choices, T. Rowe Price Mid-Cap Growth. Cohn recommends she spread her money among several stock funds. "She may not think her nest egg is large enough to diversify," says Cohn, "but that's still 100% of her assets right now."

Cohn suggests an equal division among four of the T. Rowe Price funds offered by the plan. In addition to Mid-Cap Growth, they include Equity Income, New Horizons and International Stock. "These four funds," he says, "give you large, small and midcap domestic stocks plus internationals." Scott is looking forward to 2001, when she will have paid off her student loan and can boost her 401(k) contributions to 15%.

share of your company's matching funds the longer you stay in the plan. Schedules vary. But federal law usually requires full vesting after no more than seven years.

Your benefits counselor can tell you how soon you can sign up. At most companies, you first have to be on the payroll for a year. President Clinton recently made a number of proposals for expanding 401(k)s, including one that would encourage companies to eliminate the waiting period. Because of election-year gridlock, however, it's unlikely any changes will be enacted soon.

Why you should invest to the max. Don't think you have to wait until you're bringing home a big paycheck to start building your 401(k). Even someone earning an entry-level salary can end up with a million. The key is to start early. Say you are 25 years old with a job that pays $25,000 a year. If you save 6% of your salary, or just $125 a month, get a 50% match and earn 8% on that money, you would end up with $1.1 million by age 65. (That's assuming you get steady annual wage hikes.) And scraping together even a few dollars more can give you a surprisingly big payoff. If you're able to put away 8% of your pay, your account would balloon to $1.4 million by your 65th birthday.

You typically can set aside 15% of your salary up to the IRS maximum of $9,500 a year. That amount is increased periodically for inflation. But some employers cap your contributions at 10% of salary or less mainly to comply with complex IRS regulations aimed at making sure plans don't disproportionately benefit a company's best-paid employees. Even if you can't afford to part with 10% or 15% of your paycheck, try to come up with enough to qualify for your employer's top matching contribution. You usually can invest your employer's money in the same way you deploy yours, though some employers require you to keep their share in the company's stock. About 20% of employers also allow workers to make after-tax contributions. That means you pay normal income taxes on the money before it goes into your account. Although companies rarely match after-tax

A Family Needs to Invest for the Future

"I'd like to invest more," says Stanley Farmer, 49, a vice president with Bank One in Phoenix. "But I also like other things." Those things that appeal to Stan and wife Mary Elizabeth, 41, tend to add up. They range from $1,100 a month for childcare for the four children, ages three to seven, to the family's $2,500 annual trips and a $16,000 Champion Bass fishing boat. Like most Americans, the Farmers spend virtually all they earn, saving a paltry 5% of their $103,000 income.

That's not nearly enough for a couple looking to retire in 16 years on $80,000 a year. True, Stan has stockpiled $180,000 in his 401(k) at Bank One, and Mary Elizabeth, an assistant to an Arizona Superior Court judge, has $35,000 in the tax-deferred Arizona State Retirement Fund. But they will come up short, warns Bala Cynwyd, Pa. planner Alan Cohn, with both retirement and college.

First move? Take maximum advantage of Stan's 401(k). He now stashes only 6% of his $73,000 annual salary and bonus, though the company permits contributions of up to 12% and matches the first 20% of deposits dollar for dollar. By not maxing out, Stan kisses off $876 a year of the company match. If he upped his saving to 10%, calculates Cincinnati financial planner Michael Chasnoff, he'd bulk up the nest egg by $156,200 by the time he reaches 65, assuming an 8.5% return. Mary Elizabeth already contributes the maximum in her plan, currently 3% of her $30,000 salary.

To put an extra 4% of Stan's pay (or $2,920) into the 401(k), the Farmers must trim spending. Because contributions are pretax, kicking an extra $243 per paycheck into the 401(k) will leave the Farmers with only $175 less to spend. Stan could raise his eventual take by investing more 401(k) assets in a diversified stock fund. He now has 40% of his money in the plan's large-company stock fund, 40% in its bond fund and 20% in Bank One stock. Chasnoff suggests putting most of Farmer's 401(k) into the stock index fund and the remainder into the bond fund. That, says Chasnoff, could boost Stan's expected annual return from 8% to 8.5%.

The planners point out that aggressive investors in many other 401(k)s might aim for returns above 10%. But the investments in Stan's 401(k) don't offer much hope of that. The plan has only a money market fund, bond fund, company stock fund, large-company fund and an index fund, all run by Bank One. Says Chasnoff: "It's one of the weaker plans I've reviewed." He recommends that Stan lobby his company for funds invested in small and mid-size companies and an international selection.

contributions, they can be a handy way to boost your savings. And you're generally free to withdraw them at any time without paying a penalty.

Exercise your plan's fund options. Once you figure out how much to save, your next step is to decide where to put the money. Chances are you'll have plenty of attractive choices thanks mainly to Labor Department guidelines that encourage companies to provide a broad range of investment options. The typical 401(k) offers six funds, compared with only three or four five years ago. The mix might consist of a money-market fund, a "stable value" account or bond fund, a balanced fund, a growth fund, an aggressive growth or small-company fund, and an international fund. Some large corporations give you access to 35 or more funds. The funds that are available can be either retail funds (the kind open to all investors) or private accounts managed by banks, insurance companies and money-management firms. The retail funds are becoming more common because fund companies are bidding aggressively to capture 401(k) business. Employers also like the idea of being able to provide brand name funds their employees may recognize. The advantage of retail funds is that, by law, they must provide investors with extensive information, including the name of the manager or managers and a detailed prospectus that describes the fund's expenses and investment policies. In contrast, most private funds are not required to disclose that much detail about their operations.

Track the progress of your account. By law your employer is required to give you an account statement only once a year if you request one. (For tips on deciphering this document, refer to "Shield Your 401(k) From Foul Ups" starting on page 104). The majority of plan sponsors provide quarterly reports. And 58% let you get information on your account, including its current value and the latest performance of your funds, via a toll-free 800 number. Many large plans also allow you to change your investment choices or move money from

Ready to Retire and Reel in $500,000

When his company launched its 401(k) plan almost 11 years ago, Bob Johnson saw an irresistible deal. "I invested the maximum 15% from the start," says Johnson, a 59-year-old salesman for Wace, a Chicago design and print firm. Saving that much wasn't easy. But the family agreed to stick to budget restaurants and postponed trading in their five-year-old car. "I thought giving up some luxuries would be worthwhile down the road," says Johnson.

Today Johnson presides over $317,000 in his 401(k), placing him among the wealthiest 7% of all 401(k) investors. If he keeps pumping 15% of his roughly $60,000 salary into the plan (with Wace matching 5% of his salary) and his stash grows 8% annually, Johnson will reach $447,500 within three years. At that point, the salesman intends to ease into a part-time role for a few years before kicking back for good with his homemaker wife Caryl, now 55. They anticipate a life of golf, fishing, cross-country skiing and indulging four grandkids. Counting their 401(k), $8,500 annual Wace pension, the roughly $23,500 a year they expect from Social Security and the income thrown off by a $50,000 IRA, the Johnsons can depend on at least $31,000 a year well into their nineties.

Before that, however, Johnson must think about the potential for a stock market downturn. That's a risk he worried less about when he was a decade away from retiring. Now, however, with $317,000 to protect and only three working years left to make up losses, Johnson is nervous about the cost of a market dip. If he fails to scale back his exposure to stocks and the market slips 15%, Johnson's 401(k) account could lose $50,000. That would take nearly two years to recoup.

Financial planners Alan Cohn of Bala Cynwyd, Pa. and Michael Chasnoff of Cincinnati think Johnson should finesse this risk by moving his stash into the plan's other, more conservative investment options. Instead of providing employees individual funds to combine into portfolios that suit their needs, the Wace plan offers four ready-mixed portfolios, each a blend of six to nine stock and bond funds. The plan also offers a stand-alone money market, a stable-value option and a stock index fund. Johnson spread his money across three of the pre-blended alternatives in a mix that sinks about 76% of his total 401(k) assets into stocks. Chasnoff recommends moving 100% of Johnson's 401(k) money into the Balanced Investor portfolio. It consists of large-company stocks, small-company stocks, real estate, U.S. and foreign bonds and international stocks. That mixture will essentially cut Johnson's risk by half.

Shield Your 401(k) From Foul Ups

Common errors include contribution data deleted, withdrawals credited to the wrong person and money invested in the wrong funds. The best way to make sure none of these mishaps does permanent damage to your account is to read your quarterly statement carefully. To help you, we've printed a sample statement at right with specific tips on what to look for. Pay special attention to the earnings column, where many mistakes occur. That's mainly because many plans' record-keeping systems compute earnings indirectly. They compare the opening and closing balances, factor in all deposits and withdrawals, and then assume that the difference represents earnings. If any transaction was overlooked or counted twice, the earnings figure will be inaccurate. If you spot an error, point it out to your benefits office. If the problem still hasn't been corrected by the time you get your next statement, complain in writing to your benefits office and the plan administrator.

Miscues can also occur as you take money out of the plan when changing jobs or at retirement. If you think that you've been short-changed, try to resolve the problem with your employer. If you are unable to settle the dispute after a couple of months, consider calling the National Center for Retirement Benefits (800-666-1000), a private firm. The NCRB's "pension detectives" will examine your account and try to get your money back. The price may be high, with the company keeping as much as 50% of whatever it recovers for you. But NCRB may be able to net you more than a lawyer would.

Your money is usually safe even if your company goes broke because your account is held in trust. But bankruptcy and fraud often go hand in hand. In a recent 12-month period, the U.S. Department of Labor opened over 650 criminal and civil fraud investigations of 401(k) plans, up from about 75 the year before. Most problems involved financially troubled small companies that may have tapped participants' money to pay their bills. Your best defense against outright thievery is to scrutinize your statement. Make sure your contributions are being deposited promptly. By law, your employer has 90 days to transfer the money withheld from your paycheck into your account. And look for records of unauthorized loans or withdrawals. If you spot something suspicious and you can't get a satisfactory explanation from your employer, your next step is to call a pension adviser at the DOL's Pension and Welfare Benefits Office in Washington, D.C. (202-219-8776).

Your 401(k) Plan

[Account statement for the quarter ended March 31, 1996]

The basics: Don't overlook this routine information; minor errors here can create major tax headaches when you take distributions from your plan.

Vesting: This refers to the percentage of the company's contributions that you can take with you if you decide to leave. Your benefits department can tell you about your company's vesting policy.

Opening balance: Make sure this matches the closing balance from your previous statement.

Loan repayments: These should be invested the same way as your regular contributions.

Transfers: Transfers between funds in your account should always add up to zero.

Closing balance: Even simple calculations can be wrong, so double-check the math. Start with the opening balance and add in all the activity for the quarter. The result should equal the closing balance.

YOUR NAME
123 Main Street
Yourtown, State 01234
Date of Birth: 2/3/65
Social Security number: 123-45-6789

Date of enrollment: 1/1/91
Vesting percentage: 60%

Deferral percentage
Before-tax: 6%
After-tax: 0%

Investment elections:
Balanced fund: 30%
Growth fund: 60%
Company stock fund: 10%

	COMPANY STOCK FUND	BALANCED	GROWTH FUND	TOTAL
Opening balance	$6,964.20	$13,145.02	$16,413.58	$36,522.80
Contributions				
Before-tax	$55.38	$166.14	$332.28	$553.80
After-tax	$ —	$ —	$ —	$ —
Company match	$27.69	$83.07	$166.14	$276.90
Earnings	$138.70	$633.96	$1,350.72	$2,123.38
Loan repayments	$68.53	$205.58	$411.16	$685.27
Transfers	−$100.00	+$100.00	$ —	$ —
Withdrawals	$ —	$ —	$ —	$ —
Distributions	$ —	$ —	$ —	$ —
Closing balance	$7,154.50	$14,333.77	$18,673.88	$40,162.15
Shares/Units	257.820	8,896.106	10,374.378	
Share/Unit price	$27.75	$1.61	$1.80	

Loan summary
($5,000 borrowed at 9%)

Beginning balance	$3,832.70
Principal paid	$603.52
Interest paid	$81.75
Outstanding balance	$3,229.18

Some Bank, Trustee

Loan summary: Compare these figures to the loan-repayment schedule that you should have received when you borrowed the money to make sure your payments are being credited properly.

Withdrawals and distributions: Any money you have taken out of your account will be recorded here; the figures should agree with the statement you received when you got your payouts.

Deferral percentage and investment elections: Verify that these figures reflect the amount you want to contribute and how you want the money to be invested.

Contributions: The total should reflect your deferral percentage. If, for example, you earn $36,920 a year and are kicking in 6% of your salary, your quarterly contribution should equal $553.80 (36,920 x 0.06 ÷ 4 = 553.80).

Earnings: Your earnings should correspond to the performance of the funds you are invested in. To find out how those funds did, however, you'll have to consult the separate quarterly performance update that accompanies your account statement. Here's a quick system for checking: for each investment, divide your earnings by the average of your opening and closing balances. If you have not made any large transfers or withdrawals during the quarter, the result should roughly match the investment's quarterly percentage gain or loss.

one fund to the other whenever you like. While that flexibility is a nice perk, don't get carried away with it. Remember that your 401(k) is a long-term investment. There's no need to be constantly fine-tuning your portfolio. For more on how to invest your money, see "Perfecting Your Plan's Fund Mix" on the next page.

Keep a sharp eye on expenses. There is no law requiring that all plan expenses be disclosed to the participant. Moreover, financial services companies often make pricing complicated by, say, levying different charges depending on the number or type of transactions that plan participants actually make. Even the people in charge of your plan may be in the dark. A survey by Dalbar Associates, a Boston market research firm, found that 78% of plan sponsors did not know the investment management expenses of their 401(k) plans. And that ignorance may account for the fact that plan costs vary as widely as the plans themselves do. One survey found that 401(k) plans with 1,000 participants and $20 million in assets rang up costs ranging from $119 per employee to $518.

About 80% of those expenses are investment management fees that come out of your account, reducing your earnings. While most companies will pick up the administrative costs, some tap employee accounts for those fees as well. So what is a reasonable amount to pay? In general, you should pay no more than 1% in total costs. Keeping costs that low can be difficult if your 401(k) offers retail funds, however. That's because you may be paying investment management fees that are twice those of other accounts. For example, expense ratios for retail U.S. stock funds with $100 million or more in assets average about 1.2%, compared with 0.5% for a comparable institutional fund. Fund companies are piling up profits on their 401(k) business by levying a retail expense structure on institutional accounts, where the costs are significantly lower.

Lobby hard for plan improvements. If there are aspects of your 401(k) that seem unsatisfactory, you can't afford to ignore them and neither can the people who sign your paycheck. By law your employer is a fiduciary of the plan. That means your company has an obligation to offer as good a plan as reasonably possible and manage it prudently on your behalf. Indeed, plan sponsors have voiced concern that they may be sued in the future by employees who fail to amass enough money in their 401(k)s to fund a comfortable retirement. So chances are your company will at least consider your complaints.

To get the ball rolling, write your benefits department and explain exactly how you would like to see your plan improved. For instance, if you don't know how much your 401(k) is costing you, ask your benefits officer to explain exactly what the fees are. If you aren't happy with the answers, suggest hiring a benefits consultant to compare the costs and options in your plan with others on the market. If you aren't supplied with information about your privately managed account, ask for detailed reports like those that retail funds distribute. If the plan provider will not cooperate, urge your company to find another one. With all the competition in the 401(k) market today, companies can get excellent plans that will keep employees informed about their investments and costs. It may also help to enlist the support of high-ranked executives, who probably have even more money in the 401(k) plan than you do. For added ammunition, identify the bottom-line advantages to the changes you would like. For example, if your company saddles employees with the plan's administrative fees, you should point out that those costs are tax deductible for the corporation but not for plan participants. Above all, be persistent. Your efforts may make a great investment even better.

Perfecting Your Plan's Fund Mix

Of all the decisions employees face in managing their 401(k)s, investing the money often provokes the highest anxiety. But it doesn't have to. Making the most of the investment options in a 401(k) isn't that complicated. You can boil the process down to some simple steps. And you don't need to be a genius at choosing top funds. Nor do you have to develop a psychic ability to call the precise moment to get into or out of the market.

For all the attention given those alleged skills, an influential study by money managers Gary Brinson and Brian Singer and consultant Gil Beebower showed that fund picking and market timing don't matter nearly as much as how you mix the basic building blocks of a portfolio. These include large-company or small-company stock funds, international funds, bond funds, and cash investments such as money-market and stable value funds. According to the study, asset mix determines more than 90% of the difference in how any two portfolios perform. The specific securities you choose account for less than 5% of that difference. If anything, asset allocation is even more important in a 401(k) plan, which will typically include funds representing half a dozen different types of assets but with only one or two of each type. After all, even if you were to have a knack for picking the year's top small-cap fund, it wouldn't do you much good if your 401(k) plan offers only one. So the key to a winning strategy is quite simple. Choose the right asset mix and stick to it. These steps will set you on the right course.

Train yourself to think long term. This may be the hardest part of the whole process. To be a true long-term investor, you have to ignore the constant chattering in the business news about which funds are hot and whether the market will be up or down next week or next month. You also have to ignore the occasional visceral urge to run for the hills when the market takes a nosedive. That's harder. But it's part of the job description too. The longer your time horizon, the stronger the case for investing in your plan's stock funds, which is where you'll get the best returns. Since 1926, large-company stocks have returned almost 11% annually, close to double the 5.3% gain for intermediate-term government bonds, according to Ibbotson Associates. The problem is that stocks are much more nerve-racking than bonds in the short run. In 1974, large-company stocks' worst year of the past three decades, they lost a sickening 27% of their value. Intermediate-term bonds lost only 5% in their worst year, 1994.

The thing to remember is that a single year's loss doesn't matter much if you are looking ahead 10 years or more. You'll have ample opportunity to make up for it. If you're drawing closer than 10 years to retirement, don't confuse the end of your career with the end of your investing horizon. You will need your money to grow well beyond your retirement date, perhaps up to your death. Consider that the life expectancy of the typical 55-year-old woman today is more than 82 years. That means a portion of her cash must last at least 27 years. By any measure, 27 years is long-term investing.

Be honest about your stomach for risk. It's one thing to understand the theory that most investors should keep their 401(k)s primarily in stock funds for long-term growth. It's quite another to act on that theory when the market is in free-fall and your nest egg is shrinking 10% or 20% before your eyes. So level with yourself regardless of how far off your retirement may be. If you lie awake nights when stock prices dive, don't put as much into stock funds as your time frame alone might suggest. Instead, you should cushion your portfolio with a larger helping of bonds. But beware of investing too conservatively. You may be overlooking the bite of inflation. An investor who put $1,000 in a safe money-market fund 70 years ago would have an account worth only $1,500 today after inflation is taken into account. By contrast that same $1,000 invested in large-company stocks would have grown to about $129,800.

Assemble your ideal mix of assets. We asked the Vanguard Group, which manages about $60 billion in 401(k) assets, to design three model portfolios for people with varying time horizons and risk tolerances.

You'll find them explained in "Smart Ways to Invest Your Stash" at right. If none is a perfect fit, pick the one closest to your age and customize it. Consider the portfolio designed for a typical 25-year-old. Some people in that age group may well conclude that the portfolio's historic return of nearly 12% a year over the past 25 years isn't worth the chance of repeating a loss of 28% in a single year. They might decide instead on a blend of 80% stocks and 20% bonds. That portfolio's worst yearly loss was a more bearable 22%.

Your employer may offer a sort of prefab portfolio called an asset allocation, or a lifestyle fund. About 9% of plans now have one, up from less than 1% two years ago. Lifestyle funds follow a preset asset mix aimed at a particular stage in a person's life. One that's designed for younger investors (who have a long time horizon) might hold a steady 80% stock, 20% bond mix, while one for middle-aged investors might be 60% in stocks and 40% in bonds. If your employer offers this option, don't go for it. The problem with one-size-fits-all is that you tend to get a bad fit. You'll do better to tailor your 401(k) to one of our recommended mixes or one of your own devising.

Take the best your plan has to offer. Once you've decided on an overall mix, check out the specific choices your employer offers. In a typical plan, your choices include stock and bond funds, your company's own stock, a money-market fund and a so-called stable value account sponsored by a bank or insurance company. Your 401(k) plan may not offer every type of fund you see in our model portfolios. But it could someday soon. About 46% of plans now have an international or global stock fund, up from a mere 14% two years ago. In the meantime, substitute the closest available option. Here's how the 45-year-old model portfolio could be divvied up.

If your plan doesn't offer a large-company fund, find out which one most closely fills the bill by asking about what's called median market capitalization. Market cap is determined by multiplying a company's stock price by

Smart Ways to Invest Your Stash

These three model portfolios were designed for 401(k) investors at distinctly different stages of their careers. One of them may fit you right off the rack. Or you may want to tailor the closest one to better fit your age and risk tolerance. If you're risk-shy, you can lighten up on stocks and put more money into bond funds instead. For each portfolio, we show annual returns for a recent 25-year period as well as the best and worst years for the allocations.

For 25-year-olds, an aggressive mix
[100% stocks]

Annual return	Best year (1980)	Worst year (1974)
12%	35%	−28%

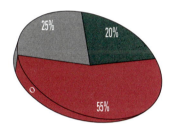

- 🟥 Large-company stock funds
- ⬜ Small-company stock funds
- 🟩 International stock funds

For 45-year-olds, a moderate blend
[80% stocks, 20% bonds]

Annual return	Best year (1975)	Worst year (1974)
11%	31%	−22%

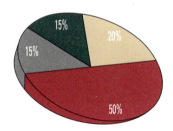

- 🟥 Large-company stock funds
- ⬜ Small-company stock funds
- 🟩 International stock funds
- ⬜ Intermediate bond funds

For 55-year-olds, a less risky recipe
[60% stocks, 40% bonds]

Annual return	Best year (1975)	Worst year (1974)
10%	28%	−18%

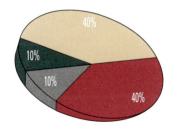

- 🟥 Large-company stock funds
- ⬜ Small-company stock funds
- 🟩 International stock funds
- ⬜ Intermediate bond funds

Sources: The Vanguard Group, Lipper Analytical Services

the number of shares outstanding. For a fund that buys mostly large-company stocks, the answer should be $5 billion or more. If that question proves too difficult for your benefits department, ask about the fund's 10 largest stockholdings. A host of familiar names like IBM, Philip Morris and General Electric indicates the fund favors large companies. Other tip-offs are funds labeled blue chip, growth and income or S&P 500 index. One word of warning. No matter how much you like the company you work for, don't bet your retirement on its stock. Experts say the absolute maximum you should invest in any single stock is 10%. If you find you have more company stock than that, ask your plan administrator whether you can move the excess into a more diversified stock fund. If anybody asks, you aren't being disloyal, just prudent.

If your plan doesn't have a small-company fund, look for one with a median market cap of $1 billion or less. Funds labeled aggressive growth often hold a healthy share of small stocks. If your plan doesn't offer such a fund, stick this slice of your portfolio into a large-company fund instead. Ditto if your 401(k) offers no funds with international or global in their names. If your plan doesn't have an intermediate-term bond fund, a general bond fund that holds issues of all maturities, from one to 30 years, would be the next best thing. If your plan lacks any kind of bond fund, a stable value account would be a fair substitute. Stable value accounts typically consist of contracts, issued by insurance companies or banks, that promise to pay a set rate of interest for a certain period, often two to five years. The accounts usually offer higher yields than money-market funds by one percentage point or more a year. Before you invest in one, check that it's diversified among at least five different issuers or otherwise protected against the risk of default. If you have none of those options, use a money-market fund.

Make adjustments in your account. Check your 401(k) portfolio once or twice a year and, if necessary, bring it back into line with the asset mix you've chosen. If stocks rose, say, 30% in value in the past year while bonds went up only 10%, you'll find that you have more in stock funds and less in bond funds than your model portfolio calls for. To keep things in balance, shift money out of the stock account and into bonds. That said, don't fall prey to the impulse to change investments willy-nilly. Trying to time the market by jumping from stocks to bonds or vice versa at the right moment is a game most pros lose. A good mix of assets will prosper over the long term. But it won't guarantee great returns every month along the way. So strive to ride through the bad patches, keeping your eye on your long-term goal of a prosperous retirement.

Tap a 401(k) While You're Working

It's easy to get your hands on your 401(k) funds if you understand the rules. For example, you can withdraw money from your account while you're working only if you're suffering a financial hardship. Yet you can always borrow against your account if your company allows loans. In fact, at any given time 20% of 401(k) participants are borrowing against their plans. Once you're retired and older than 59.5, you can take money out of your plan without owing tax penalties. Taking money out, however, makes sense only if you're very careful and really need to do so. After all, extracting money from your 401(k) means thumbing your nose at an immediate tax shelter, siphoning off your retirement savings, possibly forgoing investment earnings plus perhaps boosting your current tax bill. Still, sometimes pulling money out can be a handy way to help reach other financial goals.

Deft ways to borrow from your plan. Promise yourself that you won't succumb to temptation and pull money out of your 401(k) just to have more spare cash on hand. But you may have a legitimate reason such as buying a new home to take money out of your account. There are two options—loans and hardship withdrawals.

The Rundown on Retirement Plans

PLAN	AVAILABLE TO	BEST FOR	MAXIMUM CONTRIBUTION
401(k)	Employees of for-profit businesses	Everyone who qualifies	15% of salary, up to $9,500[1] in 1996
403(b)	Employees of nonprofit organizations	Everyone who qualifies	20% of gross salary or $9,500, whichever is less
IRA	Anyone with earned income	Those who don't have company pension plans or who have put the maximum into their company plans	100% of wages up to $2,000; $2,250 if joint with spouse
SEP	The self-employed and employees of small businesses	Self-employed person who is a sole proprietor	13% of net self-employment income, or $22,500, whichever is less[2]
PROFIT-SHARING KEOGH	The self-employed and employees of unincorporated small businesses	Small-business owner who is funding a plan for himself and employees	Same as SEP[2]
MONEY-PURCHASE KEOGH	Same as profit-sharing Keogh	Small-business owner who wants to shelter more than allowed by profit-sharing Keogh	20% of net self-employment income, or $30,000, whichever is less[2]
DEFINED-BENEFIT KEOGH	Same as profit-sharing Keogh	Self-employed person nearing retirement who needs to set aside a high percentage of income	Maximum needed to fund $120,000[1] annual benefit, or three years' average income, whichever is less[2]
VARIABLE ANNUITY	Anyone	Someone who has put the maximum into other plans and won't need the money for 10 years	None
FIXED ANNUITY	Anyone	Someone who has put the maximum into other plans and shuns risk	None

Notes: [1]Amount increases yearly with inflation rate. [2]Small-business owners fund the SEPs and Keoghs of their employees. [3]Percentage of employee's contribution [4]Some plans charge $20 to $30 annual administrative fees. [5]Surrender charges last six to eight years and typically decline by 1% a year. [6]All plans are subject to 10% income tax penalty, except in case of death or disability.

TAX BREAK ON CONTRIBUTIONS/ EARNINGS	MATCHING CONTRIBUTIONS	CHARGES/FEES	EARLY WITHDRAWAL[6]	NUMBER OF INVESTMENT OPTIONS
Yes/Yes	Anywhere from 0% to 100%,[3] but typically only up to 6% of salary	Depends on plan/annual expenses of 1% to 1.5% of assets[4]	Only in case of hardship	Three to 10, typically, depending on your employer's plan
Yes/Yes	Generally not available	Depends on plan/annual expenses of 1% to 3% of assets	Only in case of hardship and employee contributions only	One to 10, typically, depending on your employer's plan
Sometimes/Yes	None	Depends on investment/ zero to $50 annual fee	Always permitted	Nearly everything except real estate, collectibles and other hard assets
Yes/Yes	None	Depends on investment/ $10 to $30 a year	Always permitted	Same as IRA
Yes/Yes	None	Depends on investment/ up to $2,000 in annual administrative expenses	Always permitted	Unlimited
Yes/Yes	None	Same as profit-sharing Keogh	Always permitted	Unlimited
Yes/Yes	None	Depends on investment/ $2,000 to $4,000 annual expenses	Always permitted	Unlimited
No/Yes	None	6% to 8% surrender charges[5]/annual expenses of 2% to 2.2% of assets	Always permitted	Anywhere from one to 22, but typically nine
No/Yes	None	Surrender charges of 6% to 8%[5]	Always permitted	One

Roughly 80% of companies with 401(k) plans now let employees borrow as much as half the money in their accounts to a maximum of $50,000. If your company permits it, you can even have more than one loan going at the same time as long as your outstanding debt does not exceed the limits. Some employers allow loans only for serious purposes, such as buying or remodeling a home. But nine out of 10 plans that allow loans let you borrow for any reason at all.

Borrowing is much smarter than simply withdrawing cash. With a loan you eventually replace the money in your own tax-sheltered account. You have five years to repay the loan or, if you're using the money to buy a home, as long as 30 years. Loans let you avoid owing the immediate taxes due on withdrawals and the 10% penalty for nonretired people younger than 59.5. A 401(k) loan also tends to be one of the least expensive ways to borrow today. The interest rate is generally one or two percentage points above the prime lending rate. By contrast, banks typically charge six or more points over prime for personal loans.

There are two major drawbacks to such a loan. First, borrowed 401(k) money earns only the interest you pay yourself, not the higher returns the cash might earn if you had kept it invested in the plan. The other problem is that to keep a loan you normally must keep your job. Fewer than a third of employers with 401(k) loan provisions let former workers continue making installment payments. If you quit or get laid off, you may have to pay off the entire loan within three months. If you default on the loan, the IRS will treat the unpaid balance as a withdrawal that's subject to income taxes and a 10% penalty if you're under 59.5 and haven't retired. A large unpaid 401(k) loan balance could even push you into a higher tax bracket.

Given these risks, homeowners needing cash for important expenses like college or medical emergencies ought to consider a home equity loan instead. With a home equity loan, your interest rate won't be much higher than a 401(k) rate. And unlike a 401(k) loan, interest on a home equity loan is usually tax deductible. As a result, your money is almost certain to earn more if left in the plan than it will cost you, after tax, to borrow against your home. Say you're in the 28% federal tax bracket and you pay 5% in state and local taxes. A 9.7% home equity loan costs you just 6.5% after your deduction. You should be earning more than that on your 401(k) investments.

Make sure to remix your portfolio. Also remember that by taking out a fixed-rate loan on which you pay interest to yourself, you're effectively adding a fixed-income investment to your 401(k) account. You may therefore need to remix your plan's portfolio to make up for the low return on the loan. Ask your benefits department how the company will debit the loan. Some employers deduct it from your least speculative investments. But it's more commonly drawn proportionately from all the funds in your account. Then, if necessary, adjust your portfolio to keep the investment mix on track with your goals and risk tolerance. Here's an example. You have a $20,000 account balance—half in a stock fund, 25% in a bond fund and 25% in a guaranteed investment contract (GIC). You want to borrow $5,000 drawn proportionally from the funds. To keep the same investment mix, you should put two-thirds of the remaining GIC balance, or $2,500, in the stock fund and the other third, or $1,250, in the bond fund. That way you again have $10,000 in the stock fund, $5,000 in the bond fund and $5,000 in a fixed-income investment.

Let's say that a financial emergency strikes, and you need cash. But you have maxed out on borrowing, or your employer doesn't offer loans. Fortunately, 92% of employers with 401(k)s permit early withdrawals for financial hardship. Most stick to four hardship exemptions cited in the tax code. The four are paying college tuition for yourself or a dependent; purchasing your primary residence; covering any out-of-pocket medical costs; and preventing foreclosure or eviction from your primary residence. Some 18% of plans permit other hardship withdrawals such as for funeral expenses or child support.

The real cost of tapping your account. The ability to withdraw money from your 401(k) provides a comforting safety net. But it's a pricey option that should be used only as a last resort. Keep in mind that this is an irreversible move. You can't replace the money later on. What's more, you'll owe income taxes on the amount you take out of the 401(k) and probably the 10% penalty for early withdrawal. Worst of all, by law your employer must withhold 20% up front for taxes. To receive the money you really need, you have to take out 25% more than you want. When you file your tax return, you'll get credit for the 20% you paid. But you'll have to ante up any additional taxes that are due. To get your hands on an immediate $10,000, for example, you'd need to withdraw $12,500. Next April, if you're in, say, the 28% federal income tax bracket and pay 5% in state and local taxes, you would owe an additional $1,000 in taxes plus a 10% penalty of $1,250. And don't overlook $625 in state and local taxes. So the amount you'd ultimately keep from a $12,500 withdrawal would be just $7,125, or 57% of what you took out of your plan. (The withdrawal penalties are waived if you are 55 or over and have retired early.)

Rather than forcing your employer to act as a private investigator and prove that you have no other source for the money, the IRS okays hardship withdrawals as long as your company prohibits you from contributing to your 401(k) for a year after making a withdrawal. As a result, during that time, you forgo not just your tax-sheltered salary deduction but also any employer match as well. Given all these drawbacks, if a cash crunch hits, you'd probably be better off dipping into your emergency funds or getting a loan from your family and friends.

What to do when you change jobs. Don't make the most common 401(k) mistake—taking your entire account in cash rather than reinvesting it in another tax-deferred plan. (Other mistakes are covered in the box at right.) A whopping 79% of workers who quit or get fired and take the cash from their 401(k) plans elect not to reinvest all of it in another plan. By failing to do so, you

Common 401(k) Mistakes You Can Avoid

Once you have identified risks that reside in your 401(k) fund portfolio, you can adjust your holdings to suit your particular investment goals and temperament. That might mean, for example, reducing your interest-rate risk by lightening up on your funds invested in long-term bonds. Then again, you may decide to shoulder new risks in pursuit of higher returns over time. Even seasoned and market-savvy investors frequently make mistakes. What follows, however, are some common 401(k) pitfalls that you should try to sidestep.

Having too much money in your company's stock. Investors who concentrate a sizable share of their assets in any single stock are courting trouble. Many make the mistake, often without even knowing it, because they invest heavily in the shares of the corporation they work for through vehicles such as profit-sharing plans.

Leaving too much money in cash. Some investors escape the perils of stock market volatility and bond defaults by keeping the bulk of their 401(k) portfolio in cash. But they often overlook the even more relentless threat of inflation. Cash equivalents such as Treasury bills, short-term bonds and money-market funds carry almost no risk—and no chance for capital gains that can outpace rising prices.

Assembling a portfolio piecemeal. You may be a genius at spotting enticingly undervalued stocks or choosing top-performing funds over the long haul. But a collection of great individual investments does not always provide the balance your 401(k) portfolio needs. If you have already loaded up on stock funds, for example, you probably should pass on that promising new fund pick that you read about and buy an income-generating bond fund instead.

Buying more investments than you can monitor. To diversify fully, you may be tempted to own so many assets that you do not have time to follow them all carefully. Or you may buy investments for which accurate information is hard to obtain. Remember that less can be more in a 401(k). Choose a mutual fund or two instead of a host of individual stocks to fill out the gaps in your diversification plan.

Overlooking important assets. Many investors focus their diversification efforts too narrowly, excluding major assets such as their rising earning power, appreciating home and mounting personal savings. But such assets may be the most valuable. If your brokerage account is stashed in long-term bonds and cash, consider tilting your 401(k) toward growth-oriented stock funds.

subject your savings to immediate taxes and the 10% penalty for withdrawals. You also jeopardize your future financial security because compounding tax-deferred money is the best way to save for retirement.

If possible, when you leave a job and a 401(k), choose instead one of the three options. You can leave your money where it is, transfer it to your new employer's 401(k) plan or roll it into an IRA. As long as your account exceeds $3,500, you can leave your money in your former employer's plan until you retire. You won't be able to contribute more to it. But the account will keep making money for you, and you can always roll over the money into a different sheltered account later. So if you need time to think over your options, this might be the best short-term move. Long term, however, there are disadvantages to leaving the money in your former employer's 401(k). For starters, you won't be allowed to borrow against the account. And since you can no longer contribute to it, the company won't match any funds. So unless the investments in your account are doing spectacularly well, don't leave your money in your old plan any longer than necessary.

If your new employer offers a 401(k), you usually can transfer your cash to that plan. You may have to wait a year or so to become eligible to make new contributions, however. Switching from one employer's plan to another is your best strategy because a 401(k) and its cousins at nonprofits are the only savings program that offer matching contributions. If you roll money into a new 401(k), however, make sure your old employer hands over the money directly to the new plan's trustee, not to you. If you are the recipient, your employer has to withhold 20% for taxes. What's more, you'll have to replace the missing 20% from your own pocket within the 60 days allowed for a rollover. Otherwise, that amount will be considered a withdrawal, subject to taxes and the 10% penalty.

An IRA is your best bet if your new company has no 401(k) plan or doesn't allow rollovers. One tip is to set up a new IRA account, sometimes called a conduit IRA, and then keep your mitts off it. If you don't mix that money with other contributions, you'll be allowed to roll it back into a 401(k) plan in the future. As with the transfer described above, make sure the money goes directly to your IRA trustee.

Taking Money Out Once You Retire

Congratulations. You've made it to age 59.5, the stage in your career in which you finally can kiss those rules regarding 401(k) early withdrawals and tax penalties good-bye. You've worked hard, endeavored to invest wisely, kept borrowing to a minimum and are ready to start enjoying the fruits of your labor in retirement.

Not so fast. When it's time to start pulling money out of your 401(k), you'll face a tangle of irrevocable tax and investment decisions that could tarnish your golden years if you mishandle them. Make the right moves, however, and your 401(k) will be your ticket to a cushy retirement. Your first step is to get help from a professional tax adviser. Says Paul Westbrook, a retirement planner in Ridgewood, N.J.: "Deciding how to handle your 401(k) at retirement is not a do-it-yourself job." To help guide you, we've laid out the seven common questions about 401(k) withdrawals in retirement and the wisest answers, according to financial planners and benefits consultants.

When do I have to start taking money out of my 401(k)? The law says you can begin making penalty-free withdrawals at 59.5, or 55 if you took early retirement. But you don't have to begin shoveling out any of the cash until you are 70.5. If you can swing it, try to draw on funds outside your 401(k) and other tax-favored accounts, letting you continue to shelter your earnings from the IRS for as long as possible.

What if my 401(k) is thriving, and my former employer will let me leave the money where it is? You probably should do just that. For one thing, this will give you even more time to map out your post-career investment strategy. "A lot of investment sharks are after this money," warns Harry Purnell, an actuary at the benefits firm Foster Higgins based in Princeton, N.J. Equally important, leaving the money in the 401(k) may offer you tax advantages that the alternative, a rollover IRA, can't match. Since the tax law limits annual pretax contributions to 401(k) plans to $9,500, some companies allow employees to contribute after-tax dollars as well. The hitch? The law won't let you put after-tax money in a rollover IRA when you retire. So if your 401(k) fund has sizable after-tax contributions, leaving the money alone is the only way to get tax deferral on your entire account. What's more, once you transfer money to an IRA, you forgo the right to elect special tax treatment available if you pocket a lump-sum payout. See "How to Reduce Your 401(k) Tax Bill" at right.

Be sure to check out your plan's rules regarding retirees' accounts in its latest summary plan description. If the information isn't there, you should ask your plan administrator for a set of written rules. Some can be restrictive. Once you leave the company, for example, your 401(k) might not let you switch among the various investment options as often as you could when you were an employee. In addition, most plans won't let you take sporadic withdrawals. Instead, they require you to take out all or nothing at all.

What if my ex-employer won't let me leave my account where it is or I'd rather invest it myself?
Move the money to a rollover IRA. You can roll the money into an existing IRA or open a new one. To do this properly, instruct your 401(k) plan administrator either to transfer the money directly by wire into your IRA or to give you a check that's made out to your IRA trustee. The distribution check shouldn't be made payable to you. If it is, you have 60 days to transfer the money into an IRA account yourself. If you don't act within 60 days, the entire amount is deemed taxable. To make matters worse, if the check is made out to you,

How to Reduce Your 401(k) Tax Bill

As this table shows, the best way to preserve your retirement nest egg from taxes is to roll over your payout into an IRA and let the fund continue to grow tax deferred. The worst is pocketing your 401(k) cash and paying ordinary income tax on the total. Our calculations assume that a 60-year-old couple with $40,000 of annual taxable income receive a 401(k) payout worth $300,000 that they wish to draw on until age 90. The after-tax amounts assume a 33% federal and state tax rate.

401(K) WITHDRAWAL OPTION	INITIAL TAX	NET SUM INVESTED	ANNUAL AFTER-TAX INCOME FROM 401(K) AGES 60 TO 65	ANNUAL AFTER-TAX INCOME FROM 401(K) AGES 65 TO 90
IRA rollover with no withdrawals for five years	$0	$300,000	$0	$27,666
IRA rollover with immediate withdrawals	0	300,000	17,854	17,854
Lump sum with 10-year averaging	81,330	218,670	14,813	14,813
Lump sum with five-year averaging	83,680	216,322	14,654	14,654
Lump sum with immediate taxation	118,640	181,360	12,286	12,286

Source: Westbrook Financial Advisers, Ridgewood, N.J. Inside the rollover IRA, the money earns a tax-deferred 8% annually. Comparable investments are made outside the IRA. But earnings on them are taxable.

your employer must withhold 20% for income taxes. So if you have a $100,000 account, you would get a check for only $80,000. To roll over the entire $100,000 within the 60-day window, you'd have to come up with the missing $20,000 on your own and add it to the $80,000 check you deposit in your IRA. Can't come up with the 20 grand? Then the tax law says you've made a taxable withdrawal of that amount. Thus you'll owe income tax on the $20,000. That's a $6,600 hit assuming a combined 33% federal, state and local tax bracket.

What are my options if I want to take my 401(k) cash now to buy the RV of my retirement dreams? If you don't want to roll over your stash, you need to plan ahead to minimize your tax hit. The best strategy for reducing Uncle Sam's bill is to use a special calculation called forward averaging. Five-year forward averaging is available to anyone 59.5 or older who has participated in his or her 401(k) for at least five years before the year of the distribution. You compute the taxes due as if you received the money over five years instead of all at once. Without averaging, a couple getting a $300,000 lump-sum 401(k) payout might owe $118,640 in taxes, assuming they had $40,000 of other income. With five-year averaging, the tax would be $83,680, or 29% less. The benefits of five-year averaging wane as your payout gets larger. Note, however, that once your distribution tops $1,318,750, five-year averaging gives you the same tax bill as the ordinary income tax calculation.

Were you born before 1936? If so, you can instead choose 10-year forward averaging, which often saves you even more in taxes. With 10-year averaging, you compute your tax as if you had received your payout over 10 years, using the tax rates for singles that were in effect in 1986. For distributions of up to $358,250, this is the way to go if you qualify. Using this example, the tax you would owe on $300,000 with 10-year averaging would be just $81,330, vs. $83,680 using the five-year method. If you take lump-sum distributions from more than one retirement plan during the year, you must apply it to all your lumps. So if you would like to roll over one of the payouts into an IRA and forward average the other, arrange to take your distributions in different years.

Here's one final caution. If you plan to use forward averaging on a lump sum exceeding $775,000 this year, you could be hit with a 15% excise tax penalty on the amount over $775,000. This is the result of so-called excess distribution rules designed to ensure that taxpayers use 401(k)s and other tax-sheltered plans to build up an adequate retirement fund, not to amass family fortunes. The threshold is adjusted periodically for inflation. If you're planning on taking $775,000 in a lump sum, see your tax adviser before you do. He or she may be able to suggest ways to avoid or mitigate the combination of taxes and penalties that you will owe.

■ **What if I'll need some, but not all, of the cash in my 401(k) soon?** Then you'll most likely want to dump your 401(k) into a rollover IRA and make taxable withdrawals as needed. But unless you have to, don't take out more than $155,000 in any single year. Here's why. If the sum of your annual withdrawals from all your tax-sheltered nest eggs exceeds $155,000, you'll get nailed with a 15% penalty on the excess in addition to the income tax. The $155,000 annual limit also adjusts for inflation but increases only in $5,000 increments.

■ **Can I get my ex-employer to give me periodic payments from my 401(k)?** That depends on whether the company is among the roughly 33% of 401(k) plan sponsors that offer an installment payment option. If it is, you select a payout period that's typically five to 15 years. Choose 10 years, and you'll get one-tenth of your balance in Year One, one-ninth in Year Two and so on until your account is depleted at the end of 10 years.

■ **What steps do I have to start taking once I reach the age of 70.5?** At this age you must begin withdrawing specified annual amounts out of all your tax-sheltered accounts. How you make these withdrawals will have income tax consequences and possibly estate tax repercussions as well. To brush up on the rules and the issues surrounding mandatory distributions, get a copy of IRS Publication 590—Individual Retirement Arrangements. It's available free by calling 800-829-3676. The minimum amount you must withdraw once you turn 70.5 is based on two factors. The first is your life expectancy as determined by IRS tables. (If you have a beneficiary, you'll use one figure representing your joint life expectancy.) The second is the total you have in each tax-sheltered account. For example, if you and your spouse are both 71, your joint life expectancy is 19.8 years. If you have a $100,000 rollover IRA, you must withdraw at least $5,050 ($100,000 divided by 19.8). You can take out more. But failure to take at least the required minimum means owing a tax penalty equal to a staggering 50% of the shortfall.

To lower your minimum annual payout, name as young a beneficiary as you can. Most people choose their spouse. But if he or she is adequately provided for through other means, naming someone younger will help both of you stretch your 401(k) money in retirement. A younger sibling raises your joint life expectancy, which, in turn, lowers your payout. The 71-year-old IRA owner in the above example would lower his mandatory payout from $5,050 to $3,950 if his beneficiary was 61 instead of 71. Suddenly feeling very generous toward your 12-year-old grandchild? Forget it. If your beneficiary is not your spouse, the IRS tables impose a maximum 10-year age spread between you and your beneficiary to prevent you from drastically reducing your payouts.

Now you'll need to select a method for calculating your life expectancy. The IRS permits two methods—recalculation and term certain. The choice you make is irrevocable, so consider your options carefully.

Under the recalculation method, the IRS uses an actuarial table to figure the life expectancy of you and your beneficiary every year. Based on the reassuring conviction that the longer you live, the longer you're expected to go on living, the recalculation method reduces your life expectancy by less than one year for each year you live. This method is appropriate if you want to stretch out your minimum payments over as many years as possible and maximize your tax-deferred buildup.

The term-certain option establishes life expectancy up front and drops it by one year every year. Thus your 401(k) is depleted sooner than if you used recalculation. You may prefer this if you want to assure yourself a stream of payouts for a definite time period but are also interested in pulling money out of your account so that you can give it as a gift to your heirs. Such gifts reduce the size of your estate and possible future estate taxes.

5

Manage Your Funds Like a Pro

*E*very day millions of Americans show a remarkable faith in the integrity of strangers, entrusting their savings to the largely anonymous money managers who run mutual funds. The industry has earned that trust during the past 50 years despite some embarrassing blemishes in the go-go funds era of the late 1960s. It has built a reputation as champion of the little guy in the often brutal global financial markets. The industry's bond with investors, however, has been eroded by recent episodes involving the abuse of derivatives, the ethics of fund managers and other troubling issues.

Industry officials contend there's no reason for concern. "These minor blips show how well we do at maintaining our standards," says Matthew Fink, president of the Investment Company Institute, the fund trade association. Yet one prominent fund watcher believes the torrent of dollars may have distracted some from their real mission. "The emphasis over the past few years seems to have moved from portfolio management to selling a product," says Kathryn McGrath, formerly the Securities and Exchange Commission's top fund regulator and now a securities lawyer in Washington, D.C. "Some people have forgotten that funds are a fiduciary business, which is disturbing." MONEY hasn't. Here are our answers to nagging questions many investors may have about funds. We believe that the insights we've gathered can help you manage your fund portfolio like a pro. After all, a smarter fund investor is ultimately a richer one.

Answers on Safety and Ethics

In the race to stand out among today's countless fund choices, an increasing number of managers invested in highly volatile securities that can boost their portfolios' returns—and also subject them to sizable losses. For example, managers of some aggressive small-cap funds bought speculative issues of new and untested companies that do not trade on major stock exchanges. In bond and money-market funds, the new big risk comes from the arcane securities known as derivatives. These are complex instruments, such as inverse floaters and structured notes, whose value is based on some underlying asset, commodity or interest-rate index. Fund ranker Lipper Analytical Services estimates that more than half of fixed-income and money funds have used some form of derivatives to hedge their bets or boost yield. When rates shot up in 1994 and early 1996, derivatives soured far faster than the pros expected. As a result, many investors were stunned by losses in supposedly conservative bond funds. What's more, in 1994 about 20 money-market funds had to be bailed out by their sponsors because of problems with derivatives.

Is my fund as safe as it claims? Bruised shareholders in some bond funds have reason to ask that question. In most cases, even a careful inspection of a fund's prospectus might not have alerted them to the potential time bombs because the disclosure is worded so opaquely. Take, for example, a gander at this section from the prospectus of one battered bond fund. "The fund may also invest in inverse or reverse floating CMOs. Inverse or reverse floating CMOs constitute a tranche of a CMO with a coupon rate that moves in the reverse direction to an applicable index such as LIBOR." Got that? Even reading a fund's portfolio might not have revealed the derivatives. Since funds are required to file their holdings only in their semiannual and annual reports, some managers engage in a technique that's called window dressing in the trade. That means dump-

What You Don't Know About Funds

MONEY recently put 20 questions about funds and investing to nearly 1,500 people nationwide who own funds directly or through retirement savings plans at work. We found that most investors are candidates for Fund Basics 101. For starters, respondents answered just half the questions correctly, for an overall score of 49 out of 100. Only 16% scored at least 70, the passing grade used by the American College in Bryn Mawr, Pa. on its test for chartered financial consultants.

Indeed, large numbers of investors are clueless about some of the most rudimentary principles of fund investing. Some 33% of those polled mistakenly thought that a fund's diversified portfolio eliminates risk, while 12% said they weren't sure if it did or not. So only slightly more than half of investors seemed to realize that while diversification can prevent losses in a single security from torpedoing a fund, it doesn't immunize a fund against overall market declines. The one question that fund investors really nailed suggests they know a lot more about dipping into their stash than investing it. Some 71% knew that 401(k)s and other employer-sponsored retirement plans often let you borrow against the money you've invested.

We should note that investors' scores were dragged down a bit by a few tough questions that could thwart otherwise savvy fund owners. Only 28% of the test takers correctly identified duration (a statistical measure of bonds' sensitivity to interest-rates) as the best indicator of how much a bond fund's value was likely to fluctuate. Nonetheless, our analysis of the poll results suggests that investors would be wise to take the following steps if they hope to manage their funds like a pro.

Learn how to evaluate fund returns. Fewer than half the people we surveyed knew that the best overall measure of a fund's performance is its total return, a yardstick that factors in dividends, capital gains or losses, plus any increase or decrease in the fund's share price. Some 27% mistakenly believed that a fund's yield was the best performance gauge; 14% thought that the income the fund paid was the most relevant barometer; and another 11% were convinced that a fund's capital-gains distributions are the best way to monitor its progress. Considering that the majority of fund investors didn't grasp the importance of total return, it's hardly surprising that only a third knew how to figure something slightly more sophisticated—a fund's real return. This shows how your fund actually did after subtracting the inflation rate from its performance during the period you're measuring.

Come to terms with risk and reward. Investors don't appreciate fully that shooting for higher returns involves taking on greater risk. Only a third knew that if two companies issue bonds with identical maturities at the same time but with different interest rates, the one whose bonds carry the higher rate is probably the financially weaker of the two. Some 44% believed that the companies' financial strength isn't relevant to the disparity in rates. Another 17% actually thought the issuer paying the higher rate is the sturdier company. "If people don't understand that there's no free lunch in the investment world, they're going to be susceptible to pitches from people selling investments that are too good to be true," says Morningstar's John Rekenthaler.

Brush up on investing strategies. Many investors apparently have serious misconceptions about key investing tenets. When we asked which type of investment historically has offered the best protection against inflation, 54% chose bonds and money-market funds over stock portfolios. Oft-quoted figures from research firm Ibbotson Associates show something quite different. Over the past 69 years, stocks have outrun inflation by roughly seven percentage points annually, vs. just two points for bonds and a measly half a percentage point for Treasury bills (a proxy for money funds). A sizable number of investors also seemed unaware of the overriding importance of asset allocation. Nearly half did not realize that the mix of stock, bond and money funds they assemble has a greater impact on their long-term returns than the individual funds they choose.

Focus more on costs and fees. Just 40% knew that stock fund expense ratios averaged between 1% and 1.5%. That's the annual costs that shareholders pay for fund management and maintenance expressed as a percentage of assets. (The exact figure for stock funds is 1.5%.) Nearly as many people thought that stock fund expense ratios averaged as high as 1.5% to 3% annually, while 21% thought expenses averaged a parsimonious 0.5% to 1%. Respondents scored the worst on our question asking what a 12b-1 fee is. Only 22% knew that it's a charge levied against the fund's assets to pay for selling the fund. Fully 38% thought that fee is part of the cost of managing the fund. Investors should avoid funds that levy 12b-1 fees. Funds that layer sales fees on top of regular operating expenses drive up the fund's costs overall and increase risk to shareholders when managers invest more aggressively to overcome the drag of higher expenses.

ing securities just before public filing dates so that they need not be reported, then buying them back later.

The only sure way to learn about your fund's use of derivatives is to question a representative directly. Remember that some derivatives can actually lower the riskiness of a fund, as when currency futures are used in a bond fund to dampen possible losses from foreign exchange fluctuations. What you want to know is whether your fund is using derivatives to pump up the fund's yield and, if so, how much the fund's value can drop if interest rates rise, say, one percentage point. Avoid funds that invest more than 5% of their assets in such derivatives. Or you can go with funds that have strict policies against or largely avoid using these derivatives. Among the standouts are Vanguard Fixed-Income Short-Term Corporate, Invesco Intermediate Government Bond, AIM Limited Maturity Treasury and Franklin Short-Intermediate U.S. Government Securities.

Is a manager looking after my interests? An unethical one could hurt a fund several ways. He could buy some stocks for his own account and then drive up their price by having the fund make huge purchases of the same stocks (a practice known as front running). In addition, a manager could accept profit-insuring deals on initial public stock offerings and feel obliged to have the fund buy other issues from the same firm regardless of whether they promise to be good investments. Or a manager could use the fund's money to invest in a firm in which friends, associates or relatives may have some financial stake. These issues surfaced when the Invesco Fund group fired star manager John Kaweske for failing to report stock trades in his personal account. Invesco insists that fund shareholders suffered no losses as a result of Kaweske's personal trading. In the wake of the incident, however, an Investment Company Institute panel issued a stringent set of new trading guidelines for fund personnel. Among the recommendations are a ban on managers' profiting from short-term transactions (buying and selling within 60 days) and investing in initial public offerings. So make sure to ask your fund whether it has adopted the tough new ICI code of ethics on personal trading. If not, you can urge it to do so or consider voting with your feet.

What about Fidelity's recent scandal? In April the *Washington Post* set off a bombshell on its front page. The newspaper reported that the SEC was investigating Jeff Vinik, then Fidelity Magellan's manager, and at least six other current and former Fidelity managers or research analysts to see whether they "traded stocks for themselves to benefit from subsequent buying or selling by Fidelity mutual funds." Such front running would be illegal as well as disturbing. In response, Fidelity said "the story is flat-out wrong." And the SEC, in an unusual step, deviated from the agency's policy of never commenting on investigations to state that "the article contains inaccuracies which have led to erroneous impressions."

What does all this mean for current or prospective Fidelity holders? First, no evidence has come forth indicating that any Fidelity employees traded improperly. Second, because of Fidelity's high profile, the SEC is likely to keep the giant firm under even closer scrutiny in the future. Third, you can be sure Fidelity, already strict, will be even more vigilant about managers' trading from now on. Unconfirmed assertions are not proof of wrongdoing. Fidelity aside, how big a problem is personal trading by fund managers? In an industry as big as the fund business, a few rogue operators will inevitably break the rules. But there are no signs of rampant abuse. Regulators and the fund companies seem to be doing a good job of policing the personal trading of the people who manage your money. Besides, you have more important things to worry about, such as your fund's performance and expenses.

How much does my fund really cost? This is basically a no-brainer if you own no-load funds. Simply look up the fund's expense ratio in the prospectus or a mutual fund rating guide such as Morningstar's or Value Line's. If the expense ratio is 1.25%, that means for every hundred dollars you have in the fund, you are paying $1.25 each year to cover the investment adviser's fee as well as marketing, advertising, custodial and administrative services. But for investors who buy funds sold only through brokers or financial planners, trying to answer this simple question can become a calculator-punching headache. Here's why. Seeking to make their commissions more palatable, many funds now offer two or three classes of shares (labeled A, B and C) with differing sales charges and annual expenses. Each share class gives you an interest in the same portfolio. But the fee structures differ, so no two classes have precisely the same net asset value or track record. A few enterprising firms, such as Paine Webber, have gone as far as D shares.

Our advice? Stick with no-loads and avoid the incredible expanding share classes. If your fund's expenses are above average, find another one or write to your fund's independent directors to ask them to bring down costs in line with the portfolio's peers.

Who's personally managing my fund? Since 1993, the SEC has required all funds to disclose the names of portfolio managers in their prospectuses and to inform shareholders whenever a manager departs. Score one for fund investors, right? Not exactly. In an irritating twist, it's getting more difficult to find out who's at the helm of many funds. That's because sponsors are still taking advantage of a regulation loophole that allows them to list multiple managers or to simply claim the fund is run by a team and give no names at all. According to Morningstar, nearly 35% of funds now say they are piloted by more than one person, up from 15% in 1989. Of course, some funds, such as those in the Twentieth Century group, really are run by an investment committee. But critics contend the team approach is often little more than an attempt to avoid revealing who is really calling the shots. Why? The fund doesn't want investors fleeing when a successful manager departs.

If your fund claims team management, ask for details such as which manager has the final say over decisions and how the team divvies up responsibilities. If the fund sponsor won't divulge this information, seek it from fund rating companies. As long as the performance is sound, it doesn't make sense to pull out of the fund over this issue alone.

Is my fund accurately priced? Fund ranker Lipper Analytical estimates that no more than 40 of the 3,800 quotes that appear in the newspaper each day are wrong, giving funds an accuracy rate of 99%. In most cases, the prices are off by a penny or two a share, usually because the fund has inadvertently mispriced one or more securities in the mad rush to meet the deadline for sending fund price data to the National Association of Securities Dealers, which distributes them to news services. This small margin of error overstates the problem, however. That's because most of the faulty net asset values (NAVs) printed in newspapers are corrected before the fund processes shareholder transactions.

A more troubling pricing problem is whether a fund is assigning the proper market value to its securities. This is mainly a concern for bond funds that hold difficult-to-price securities such as municipal bonds, junk bonds or yield-boosting derivatives. For muni bond funds, the problem is that of the 1.5 million or so issues outstanding, maybe 180 or so trade on any given day and can be priced on the basis of actual sales. That means the majority of munis are priced by matrix. This is essentially a mathematical formula that takes into account factors like the bond's coupon rate, maturity, credit rating and call features. And those that don't quite fit into a pricing formula are priced by hand. That means the fund or an independent pricing service calls several dealers to solicit so-called opinions, or estimates of the value of the bonds. Regardless of which method is used, none tells you what you would get if those bonds were sold. Similar difficulties complicate the pricing of junk bonds. If a fund's NAV is slightly inflated compared with the value of the securities it holds, such a variance is most likely to surface during times of market turmoil. The culprit could be massive redemptions that force the fund to unload its most difficult-to-price holdings. While rare, sell-offs of fund shares large enough to expose shareholders to underlying pricing problems do occur.

Pricing uncertainties are just one more reason to avoid funds that use risky derivatives. But if you want the tax-free income of muni funds, or the double-digit payouts of junk bonds, you will just have to accept the fact that the issues' prices are more like appraisals than precise reflections of the most recent sale. To lower the chances of being stung by a fund with overpriced muni or junk holdings, stick to national muni funds such as Stein Roe Managed Municipals and Tax-Exempt Bond Fund of America that tend to have the most liquid portfolios. Ditto junk funds such as Vanguard Fixed-Income High-Yield Corporate.

Who's championing my interests? Fund
investors have two principal advocates—independent directors on the fund's board and government regulators, the most prominent of which is the SEC. Independent directors, so named because they do not work for the fund company, usually meet quarterly with the fund management to weigh in on a number of issues, ranging from the size of the fund's expense ratio to the kinds of securities the fund buys. They also get together annually to review the fund's investment advisory contract. At least 40% of each board's directors must be independent (51% if the fund levies a so-called 12b-1 marketing fee). By law, the independents are there to champion the shareholders' rights, not to rubber-stamp the sponsor's requests. Still, independent directors too often go along with management on fee increases and other issues. The National Association of Securities Dealers, state securities regulators and even state attorneys general hold some sway over funds. But the SEC is the most visible watchdog for shareholders because it has the power to censure and fine funds.

Everybody Is Flogging Funds Now

No doubt you've found lots of folks eager for your business these days. There's that persistent broker who keeps calling and that smiling sales rep in your bank lobby. You may even encounter pitches for funds in such unlikely places as an airline seat, a utility bill or a newsletter from a professional organization. Here are tips on investing through brokers, banks, discount brokers, no-load families and affinity groups. Where you choose to buy should depend on how much guidance and convenience you demand. You should bear in mind, however, that hand-holders also hold out their hands. Personal advice and service will cost you more than doing the fund picking on your own.

Salesmen provide picks at a price. Investors who want advice typically turn to brokers and financial planners, who account for much of fund sales. But you have to pay for that service in the form of loads, or sales charges. These usually amount to 4% to 6% of your investment up front or a flat rate in the case of fee-only planners. There's nothing wrong with paying a load as long as the ongoing guidance and subsequent returns justify the cost. But avoid any broker or planner who pushes a fund without first learning about your financial situation, investment goals and tolerance for risk. And be sure to ask about the adviser's compensation for selling the fund. Active investors who trade frequently may prefer to work with a discount broker such as Charles Schwab and Fidelity. A key attraction is the ability to buy and sell funds with a single phone call and without the hassle of multiple applications and other annoying paperwork.

No-loads appeal to do-it-yourselfers. If you are willing to research funds on your own, it's probably a waste of money to pay a load and to miss out on the abundant no-load choices marketed directly by fund families. The first step is to write or call a fund group (most have toll-free numbers) and ask for a prospectus, an annual report and an application. You can arrange for telephone switching between funds, redemption by wire, check writing and other services. If you buy a fund on your own, of course, there is no one monitoring the account to stop you from making a mistake or to help you decide when to cut your losses or take a profit. Some no-load groups including Fidelity, Dreyfus and T. Rowe Price offer free retirement planning workbooks and assistance on asset allocation, however.

Banks sell one-stop shopping. Their target market tends to be beginning investors disappointed with returns on CDs or savings accounts. But think twice if you're tempted by higher yields. You are most likely to be offered load funds from a limited range of sponsors or a bank-run fund that may be no bargain. None of these investments is insured by the Federal Deposit Insurance Corporation (FDIC). Remember too that the convenience of a bank can be oversold. Bank-based brokers may work for outside firms and move between branches, precluding the possibility of long-term stewardship of your money.

Other marketers make their pitch. You may get a fund promotion from an organization you belong to or even a company you do business with. Nonprofits may offer so-called socially conscious funds with ethical buying criteria (for details, see "The Dilemmas of Investing in Saintly Funds" on the right). And now corporations are muscling into the fund market. American Airlines pushes its no-load American AAdvantage money fund to passengers through inflight magazines and promotional cards on food trays. Don't rush to buy a fund simply because it is offered by a group that you know. For example, the American Association of Retired Persons puts its name on a group of funds managed by Scudder. These funds are just as good as, but no better than, others in Scudder's family. Investors should judge a fund not by its name or by who is peddling it but by its long-term track record.

The Dilemmas of Investing in Saintly Funds

This year the American Medical Association released a list of 13 tobacco-related companies and 1,500 funds that invest in them. Calling tobacco "a product that has brought misery, disease, anguish and death," the AMA recommended that investors sell stocks and funds on its tobacco tally. The AMA is only the latest group to endorse socially responsible investing. There are over 40 such saintly funds that buy only companies their managers view as ethical. Consider:

Ban smoking, sexism and racism. If these represent evils to you, why not put your money where your mouth is? First, you'll have a devil of a time finding a saintly fund you fully agree with. If you're a liberal Democrat who has no beef with tobacco, you don't fit most of these funds' definitions of socially responsible. If you're a pro-choice Republican, you're just as much of a misfit. Ethical investing only sounds as if it will help you take a principled stand. If you're still buying Philadelphia cream cheese and Jello, both made by tobacco titan Philip Morris, you can't cleanse yourself of any tobacco taint by picking a fund manager who won't own Philip Morris.

When U.S. Treasuries are immoral. The standards of saintly funds can get pretty puzzling. Some refuse to buy U.S. Treasury securities because they don't want to support the military budget. But the same Treasury borrowings also fund earthquake relief. Is buying a T-bill immoral because a portion of it goes to build bombs? Once you get started with distinctions, it's hard to know where to stop. Look at Sara Lee Corp., which makes lots of things besides cakes, including Ball Park franks, Playtex bras and Kiwi shoe polish. So why did the AMA name Sara Lee one of its 13 toxic tobacco stocks? A small unit, Douwe Egberts, sells tobacco for pipes and snuff, mainly in Europe. That business makes up less than 2% of Sara Lee's $18 billion revenues.

IAI Regional's 0.00027% misjudgment. The AMA says that if you own IAI Regional Fund, you should throw it out of your portfolio immediately. This stock fund has delivered superb long-term returns at low risk. But last December, it had a grand total of 1.4% of assets in Sara Lee. With under 2% of Sara Lee's sales coming from tobacco, less than 27¢ out of every $1,000 in the IAI fund is contaminated by nicotine. Get real. A fund manager's job is to get you the best return at the lowest risk. Let the managers buy the best stocks they can find. Then, down the road, donate the proceeds to your favorite charity. You'll help a good cause and get a tax break to boot.

Just Say No to Gold-Plated Fees

A fund's future returns can't be predicted from its past performance. But history is a very reliable guide to fund expenses, which play a crucial but often overlooked role in determining how much of your fund's gains actually wind up in your pocket. These fees include any sales charges you pay when buying or redeeming shares plus investment management fees and other administrative levies you are nicked for, year in and year out. True, up-front sales charges have generally declined during the past decade, with few funds still extracting the maximum 8.5% levy. But management, marketing and administrative expenses have jumped big time.

Annual fees for stock funds overall rose nearly 50% to 1.5% of assets over a recent 10-year period. For taxable bond funds, costs spurted 13% to about 1%. Fund boosters claimed in the 1980s that fees would come down as fund size went up. Well, growth stock funds' assets have multiplied dramatically over the past decade. But average annual expenses actually rose 30% to 1.3% of assets. Those hikes would have been easier to swallow in the 1980s, when stock funds gained an average of 14% a year and bond funds rose almost 13%. But high expenses can be a real drag in the slow-growth 1990s, when returns are expected to be closer to the historic norms of 10% for stocks and 7% for bonds. If stock returns fall back to 10%, expenses would eat up 15% of fundholders' returns, vs. just 7% in the 1980s.

To see the impact of fund expenses, compare Ivy International and Harbor International, two similar funds managed by Hakan Castegren. The no-load Harbor, with its 1% expenses, rewarded investors with a recent three-year return that was 1.4 percentage points fatter per year than Ivy International's partly because of Ivy's hefty 1.5% expenses. Investors in Ivy's most popular class A shares also paid a 5.75% initial sales charge. And the reason is simple. Harbor International has long been closed to new investors. Carefully consider the following fee-related issues.

Decide whether to shoulder a load. You can avoid commissions altogether by buying your funds directly from a no-load family. That way, every dollar you invest will be working for you. If you choose to invest through a broker or financial planner, you'll most often be hit with a front load of 3% to 5% when you make your purchase. Beware of funds like Common Sense Growth that grab 8.5% of assets. If your $10,000 investment returns 10% annually over 10 years, you'll wind up with $23,735 after suffering that 8.5% sales charge, $2,200 less than in a no-load posting the same return. Newer on the scene are back loads, also known as contingent deferred sales charges. There's no fee to buy the fund. But you'll pay a stiff penalty if you cash out early, usually coughing up 1% to 5% of any withdrawal you make before the end of year five.

A growing number of broker-sold fund groups, including Merrill Lynch, now offer you the choice of buying a fund with a front or back load. While choosing between these options may be confusing, many experts say there's often little difference. That's because most back loads are accompanied by nettlesome 12b-1 fees (described in detail below), which boost annual fund expenses. You're probably best off paying a front load if you plan to hold your fund for just a few years and if the charge is 4.5% or less. Back loads tend to be more economical if your time horizon is five years or longer. While you're likely to pay a higher 12b-1 charge at the outset, in most cases it converts to a smaller service fee sometime between the seventh and ninth year.

Check out annual expense ratios. That's your fund's annual costs expressed as a percentage of its average net assets. You'll find this figure, plus a five-year expense projection, in the fee table near the front of every fund prospectus. You should generally avoid a fund if its fees are higher than the median for its investment objective. If you're torn between two funds of the same type with comparable records, you definitely should opt for the one with lower expenses.

Be on the lookout for 12b-1 fees. Named after
an SEC rule, 12b-1 fees allow funds to recoup their
advertising and marketing costs by skimming a bit from
current shareholders. These charges now range from
0.1% to 1.25% of assets per year and are included in
your fund's expense ratio. Fund companies claim that
12b-1 fees actually benefit investors by allowing funds
to gather more assets and thus spread their costs over a
bigger base, reducing expenses. But that assertion has
been challenged in a study by State University of New
York (Buffalo) finance professor Charles Trczinka. He
found that funds with 12b-1 fees don't seem to pass
economies of scale along to their investors. A fairly new
SEC rule, which was championed by the National
Association of Securities Dealers, requires funds to
include 12b-1 fees when calculating sales charges. The
rule limits annual 12b-1 fees to 0.75% of net assets but
allows funds to charge a 0.25% service fee. The measure
also caps total sales charges including 12b-1 at 6.25% to
8.5%, depending upon the fund's fee schedule.

Weigh the cost of portfolio turnover. You
might not think of turnover, or how often your fund
trades its holdings, as a significant expense. But high
turnover can cut into your returns. That's because the
fund pays a brokerage commission on each trade and,
in some cases, may actually move a stock's price with a
buy or sell decision. Each time your fund turns over its
entire portfolio (a 100% turnover rate), it costs you 0.5%
to 1%, figures Trczinka. Thus he says a fund that has a
200% turnover rate could run you $200 for each $10,000
you've invested. In addition, you'll have to pay capital
gains tax on your share of any profits the fund passes
along to you (to avoid shelling out more than your due,
be sure to consult "Trim Uncle Sam's Take" later in this
chapter). Of course, taxed gains are better than no
gains. Turnover may be an indication of appropriately
active and vigilant management, particularly in the more
volatile fund categories such as aggressive and small-
company growth.

Why You Need a Prospectus

Once you find some promising funds, take the time to phone each one to request its prospectus and most recent annual and quarterly reports. (Most funds include an application form with these documents.) Or, in the case of a load fund, you can get these documents from your broker or financial planner. Although a fund's prospectus is by design a dull read, it is full of useful facts and disclosures required by federal securities law. In general, a prospectus describes the fund's investment objectives, strategies and risks; presents statistics on its past performance; lists the sales and management fees; and explains how you can buy and sell shares.

The prospectus cover lists the fund's address and phone numbers, and in most cases briefly summarizes the fund's objectives and states the initial sales charge, if any. Though formats vary, most prospectuses are divided into a dozen or so sections. Start your examination with the section commonly called "General Description of the Fund." Ranging in length from a few paragraphs to more than a page, this section should spell out the difference between the fund's objectives and its policies (i.e., the investment strategies and techniques it is permitted to employ to achieve its objectives). These might include buying stocks on margin (using money borrowed from brokers), trading stock options or other sophisticated tactics you may not feel comfortable with.

Pay particular attention to the table usually called "Per-Share Data." This table gives the fund's annual performance over the past 10 years, or the life of the fund if it is younger than that. It shows you whether a fund's performance has been steady or erratic, and it can be used to compare a fund's year-to-year changes in share value with those of other funds with similar objectives. For example, does the fund owe much of its long-term return to one or two lucky years, or did it consistently outperform comparable funds and market barometers such as the S&P 500 index? Investors should also take the time to scan through the sections titled "How to

Purchase Shares" and "How to Redeem Shares" that explain the mechanics of getting into and out of the fund, whether by mail, phone or wire. They also tell you whether there is a sales charge; a minimum initial investment or a minimum for subsequent investments; a fee for switching from one fund in the same family to another; or a charge that may be levied for redeeming your shares.

Get to Know the Fund Manager

You aren't just acquiring shares in a portfolio of stocks or bonds when you put money in a fund. You are also paying for topnotch management—or so you hope. Thus, before committing your cash, you should learn as much as possible about the person or persons making the fund's day-to-day investment decisions. Managers come and go, and the hotshot stock picker who propelled a fund to the top of the performance charts last year may have long since left. So unless you know from reading newspapers and magazines that your fund is run by a widely respected portfolio manager, you'll want to delve into the following issues concerning the manager, whom we will refer to as Jones.

How long has Jones run the show? For all the data disclosed in a fund's prospectus and shareholder reports, you won't necessarily find the portfolio manager's name listed in these documents. But you can often learn it and how long he or she has been in charge by calling the fund. Some won't tell you because they don't want to tie their reputations to that of an individual who might leave, causing investors to pull out their money. In that case, you usually can find the manager's name and tenure in references such as Morningstar and Value Line, which are available at many public libraries. Then compare the manager's tenure with the fund's performance. You can start by checking whether the manager has been at the helm since 1990, and thus in charge during the sharp market downturn in the summer of that year as well as the bull market that began in October 1990. If so, you can probably assume that the record shows the range of the manager's investing talents. If the manager came to the fund after 1990, those skills may not have been tested in tough times.

How crucial is Jones to your returns? This

will depend largely on the fund's objectives, size and the way in which it is operated. For example, some funds have no single manager but are run instead by committees of analysts. With these funds, you should focus your attention on the team leader, if one is so designated. In general, funds that aim for aggressive growth are more apt to rely on the insights and skills of a single manager than are more conservative stock and bond portfolios. That's because aggressive growth funds typically try to take quick advantage of stock market movements and to invest in up-and-coming companies before their growth is obvious on Wall Street. To excel with this approach, a manager can't afford to wait for a cumbersome investment committee to discuss and approve which stocks the fund should buy or sell. Instead, the fund needs a decisive manager who has uncommonly good judgment and instincts. Conversely, individual expertise matters less if the fund's strategy is to invest narrowly in certain types of bonds or in the stocks of specific industries. Most specialty funds stick to stocks in their particular sector, such as electric utilities, biotechnology or healthcare providers. So their fortunes fluctuate largely in step with those of their industry no matter how talented the manager is.

How should you react if Jones leaves?

Whether you too should consider jumping ship will depend on how much influence Jones had and the fund's relative returns prior and subsequent to his or her departure. If the value of your fund starts to sink, while the market is buoyant, you will obviously want to reevaluate your rationale for this particular investment.

The Logistics of Fund Ownership

Opening a fund account is as easy as establishing a savings account at your local bank. Some funds will even let you open an account by phone if you have money in another fund in the same family and promise to send in your check promptly. Most fund applications consist of a single sheet of paper on which you supply such basic background information as your name, address, Social Security number (or taxpayer identification number) and birth date. You will be asked whether you want to open the account as an individual, which gives you alone the power to authorize switches and redemptions, or jointly with a spouse or friend. In that case, you or your co-owner can make investments on your own. But you both will have to sign all requests for redemptions and transfers of money to another fund. If you choose joint ownership, remember that in the event one of you dies, the other automatically owns all of the shares. If you buy them with someone else and leave your interest in the fund to a third person, you should instruct the fund on the application to register you and your co-owner as tenants in common. That way, if you die, the fund will transfer your rights in the fund to your designated beneficiary.

Choosing a distribution plan. Most funds require you to specify in advance what you want done with the capital gains realized in the portfolio plus the dividends and interest it generates. You have three choices. One, you can reinvest all distributions in the fund, adding to the number of shares you own. Two, you can have dividends paid to you in cash and capital gains distributions reinvested in additional shares. Or three, you can have both dividends and capital gains paid to you in cash. Unless you are an income investor, reinvestment of all distributions is probably your best choice because the newly purchased shares then begin generating capital gains and dividends. Whatever you decide, you will owe federal taxes on the distributions unless your shares are in a tax-exempt municipal bond fund or a tax-deferred account such as an IRA. Note that capital gains earned by muni bond funds are subject to federal taxes; the interest income is not.

Purchasing your fund shares. The price that you pay is the fund's net asset value per share on the day the fund receives your application. You will not receive share certificates upon investing unless you request them. There is no reason you need them unless you plan to use them as collateral for a loan. In fact, having the certificates in your possession can be an inconvenience since you will not be able to switch money to another fund or redeem shares by phone. To purchase the most shares for your money, be mindful of the date you bought them. You are better off buying shares on the day after a fund declares its dividends ("goes ex-dividend" in investment parlance). Since such payments reduce the fund's NAV, the price of shares drops by that amount.

The value of your investment technically remains the same. You neither lose nor gain because each share is worth less than before the fund went ex-dividend. But by buying in after the dividend is declared, you will avoid having to pay taxes on that particular payout. Call the fund for the dates on which it goes ex-dividend. You also can tell when a fund has declared its payout by checking the fund listings in newspaper financial pages. Usually on the day after a dividend payment has been announced, an x appears beside the fund's NAV.

When to Abandon a Sinking Ship

Deciding when to sell a fund is among the most difficult tasks of investing. It's easy to be rational in evaluating a fund before you buy it. But once your money is committed, your emotions come into play, alternately tempting you to hold on to winners long after they have peaked and to jettison losers just before they bounce back. To spot the right time to sell or switch to another fund, you must continually compare the ones you own with others and with your personal financial goals. As long as a fund is meeting your objectives, you should hold on to it. But you shouldn't hesitate to move your money if another fund seems likely to do the job better. Financial advisers say you should consider selling or switching under each of the following circumstances.

When your financial situation changes. As you get older or closer to your goals, your needs and your tolerance for risk should change. When your children near college age, for example, you should stop taking risks with your investments for their tuition because you can't afford to lose a chunk of it in a last-minute market dip. When they are in high school you should begin switching some of the college money from growth funds to short-term bond and money funds.

When the fund itself changes. Try to think back to the reasons that initially led you to invest in a fund. If it no longer fits those criteria, you should consider looking for a replacement. For example, your growth fund's assets may have grown so large that you fear the manager has lost the flexibility that helped him or her get high returns. Or your fund may have increased its annual fees beyond what you are willing to pay. You might also decide to switch if the manager responsible for the fund's past success retires or quits. Fund groups may not be in a hurry to notify investors that the manager has left. But if you notice changes in performance, volatility or the fund's investment style, a new hand may be at the helm. To find out for sure, ask the fund.

When returns lag those of similar funds. If a fund turns out to be a subpar performer, you obviously will want to replace it. Sheldon Jacobs of the newsletter *No-Load Fund Investor* suggests you give a fund at least a year to prove itself. If you are in a conservative total return fund, he adds, you might even give it two years. "Some awfully good conservative funds can drop below the averages occasionally," he says. "You have to be patient." After two years, however, it's time to take your money out of the fund if it still languishes relative to its group or benchmarks like the S&P 500 index.

Blunt the IRS' Bite of Profits

Investors' lives are greatly simplified by funds except at tax time. That's partly because tax law requires funds to pay out, or distribute, virtually all their income from interest, dividends and net capital gains each year. That means you often owe taxes on capital gains from your fund even if you didn't sell any shares. Things get more confounding when you do sell shares. If you're like most investors, you have your funds reinvest your distributions. From a tax standpoint, each reinvestment counts as a separate purchase. Thus you're confronted with a mess when you sit down to calculate your taxable gains. Included might be a large clump of shares you bought at one price (your initial investment); dozens of tiny lots acquired at different prices (shares purchased with reinvested distributions); and a further raft of small chunks each bought at yet another price (the regular purchases you made). Each lot of fund shares that you bought produces a different capital gain or loss, which means that much extra calculator punching to figure out what you owe Uncle Sam. Here are tips that can spare you some headaches.

Don't buy funds at the wrong time. Most stock funds distribute capital gains once a year, and some funds pay out income quarterly. (To learn your fund's distribution dates, call its 800 number.) If you're contemplating a purchase close to a distribution date, don't act until after the date passes. Otherwise, you'll receive a taxable payout of all the capital gains or income the fund booked since its last payout even if you've owned your stake for only a week. In effect, the fund hands you back part of your principal in the form of a distribution. But now you owe tax on it.

Check gains and losses on the fund's books.
When you're considering whether to buy a fund, check the changes in net assets in the fund's annual report. The number to look for is the "change in unrealized appreciation on investments." That represents capital gains embedded in the fund's portfolio. When the fund sells its winners, those gains must be distributed to shareholders. To judge how big the payout could be, divide the unrealized appreciation by the fund's net assets. A result of more than 0.2 suggests that a walloping big payout is possible. While the potential for a big distribution shouldn't rule out a promising fund, it could decide a close call between competing funds. In contrast, realized losses are a plus. The fund can use prior losses to offset gains for as long as eight years.

Take advantage of your losses. If one of your funds is down for the year, consider selling it and taking the tax write-off. The loss can offset capital gains plus as much as $3,000 of other income. In fact, it often makes tax sense to move out of a losing no-load fund temporarily even if you still like its prospects. The Internal Revenue Service will disqualify the loss if you repurchase shares within 31 days. But nothing prevents you from hopping into a similar fund for a little longer than that and then switching back to your favorite.

Consider cashing in the same year. While you don't want to overrule your investment sense just to streamline your taxes, here's something to think about. If you sell a fund's shares over a number of years, you have to keep records of each sale and decide which of the four IRS approved accounting methods (described below) yields the lowest tax. If you sell all at once, all four methods will give you the same tax. So you can use the simplest method called *average cost, single category.* It allows you to figure the average cost of all your shares, regardless of when you bought them. And that work will be done for you if the fund you're selling belongs to one of the growing number of families that calculate tax costs for redeeming shareholders (among them Vanguard, T. Rowe Price and Putnam). Keep in mind, however, that if you're not unloading all your shares, the single category method may cost you more in taxes than the alternatives described below.

Figure the most tax-efficient method. Unless you elect otherwise at the time you sell only some of your fund shares, the IRS assumes that the ones you sold first were the ones you bought first. That method is called *first in, first out.* It's fine if your fund has been a loser. But the oldest shares typically have the biggest gains. So they're the ones on which you're better off postponing taxes. You can do that using a method called *specific identification.* It permits you to sell whichever shares will minimize your taxes. For example, you might pick only shares on which you have a loss, thereby offsetting gains from a different investment.

The fourth method, *average cost, double category,* requires you to distinguish between shares that you've held for more than a year and those you bought more recently and to calculate a separate average cost for each. That way you can take advantage of the difference in tax rates on long-term and short-term gains. Long-term gains (on shares held more than a year) are taxed at a maximum of 28%. Short-term gains are taxed as ordinary income at rates as high as 39.6%. Here's a final caveat. Once you decide to use either single or double category for a given fund, you're stuck with that method for the fund. You are not permitted to change the tax treatment without written permission from the IRS. And don't hold your breath waiting for that.

Wield Your PC to Pick Funds

If you focus on your funds and stock holdings several times a year, a computer can help you make decisions by providing a bounty of data on performance, risks and expenses that was once available only to investment professionals. It's still up to you, of course, to supply the prudent judgment. But we show how selected software and online services can help make those judgments easier. To use these products, all you need is a modern computer ($1,200 and up in today's market), a modem ($80 to $200) and the urge to be a more successful investor.

Quicken's nifty investment upgrade. The world's best-selling financial software just got swifter via a recent upgrade, Quicken Deluxe Version 5 for Windows (call 800-624-8742 for information). The program moves well beyond its familiar turf of checkbook balancing and budget planning to become a creditable piece of investment software. To pull it off, Intuit, Quicken's manufacturer, has taken a leap online and developed a new portfolio tracker called Investor Insight. Note, however, that it's not the only reason Quicken customers might consider upgrading. The new package also adds access to online banking, an Internet browser and a number of new bells and whistles to its core banking and cash flow monitors. These features are also available in the standard version and the Macintosh editions. But only the deluxe Windows product gives you Investor Insight.

Quicken's Investor Insight competes with commercial online services like Compuserve, America Online and Prodigy as well as investment databases like Reuters Money Network. And Investor Insight leads the pack in keeping you up to date on all your fund and stock investments. Once the software is running, you specify the funds, stocks and market indexes you want to track. Then each time you fire up the program, it automatically dials a local access number and fetches data about them. For starters, you get quotes and volume information stretching back five years. By comparison, Reuters Money Network (800-521-2475) goes back only a year for historical prices. Investor Insight also retrieves any news articles concerning your investments from the Dow Jones News Service (which includes selected articles from the Wall Street Journal) and from various business press-release wires. The first time you ask about a security, you get listings of relevant news about the company dating as far back as three months. Thereafter, your file on that security is automatically updated each time you call. Investor Insight also offers Standard & Poor's research reports and industry trend summaries for an extra $5 per report.

None of the competition matches Investor Insight's facility at organizing the data into useful formats. For example, you can graph the past performance of your holdings against one another, or against any major index, simply by clicking a button. If you're curious about one of the zigs or zags that your holdings took, you can use a feature called Quick Zoom to jump to news reports for that day to find out what triggered the change. One novel feature is a text generator that prepares a written summary of price and volume moves over any time frame you choose. You also can use the new package to connect to the Internet (described in more detail below). Netscape Navigator, a World Wide Web browser, is built into Quicken Deluxe 5. This allows you to visit Intuit's and other companies' Internet sites at a competitive price.

Download market data from the Web. One part of the Internet known as the World Wide Web is a network of computers on which stock exchanges, brokerages, mutual fund companies—in fact, anyone with the right software—can construct a package of linked graphics, text and sound. Called Websites, these packages act as a kind of digital exposition booth from which companies try to inform or beguile online visitors. What distinguishes the Web from other networks is a communications protocol called hypertext. Once you enter a Website, you can simply click on a highlighted word (the hypertext) and you'll be instantly transferred to the relevant section of the same Website or to another Website originating anywhere in the world.

To get to your starting point on the Web, you launch a software program called a browser. Netscape Navigator and Mosaic are the most popular ones. You can either download them free from several Websites or buy them at a software store, if you want the manuals. You will also have to connect to the Internet. You can do that through a local access provider in your area or through a national online service like America Online and Compuserve Once you're wired, you can simply type the Web address of any of the sites that are listed below into your browser, and you'll be carried directly there. Or you can start with a directory service like Yahoo (http://yahoo.com). The Manhattan phone book of the Web, Yahoo lets you electronically search its list of 75,000 Websites worldwide. Likewise, MONEY's own site keeps an updated list of useful financial Websites.

■ **Global Network Navigator.** Now owned by giant America Online, GNN is an excellent jumping-off point for other Internet financial destinations and a creditable source of advice. It has run a series of articles on investment strategy, for instance, including one on how to divide your portfolio among various assets to get higher returns. Address: http://gnn.com.

■ **The Holt Report.** If all you want is a convenient end-of-day market summary, the Holt Report serves nicely. It lists the high, low, close and percentage change for most major indexes plus major currencies and many foreign markets. In addition to reaching it on the Web, you can sign up to have it sent to you each evening by E-mail. Address: http://turnpike.net/metro/holt/index.html.

■ **Lombard Institutional Brokerage.** To check the latest price of the funds and stocks in your portfolio, visit this site run by a discount brokerage. It offers instant quotes on most stocks, mutual funds, options and all of the major market indexes. You can also get a graph showing the price history of an investment over almost any time period. Address: http://www.lombard.com.

■ **MONEY Personal Finance Center.** Our own Website offers price quotes on 13,000 stocks, funds and indexes, background reports on the nation's 500 largest companies and new feature stories each week. Some of the features are drawn from the magazine; others are available exclusively online. Address: http://pathfinder.com/money.

Networth. If your portfolio is laden with a lot of funds, you might want to start at this site. It provides daily price quotes for most funds, as well as stocks and indexes, and permits you to search through a database of 5,000 funds for ones that meet criteria you specify. Address: http://networth.galt.com.

Securities and Exchange Commission. The SEC site contains a giant database of documents such as 10-Ks (annual financial reports) and 10-Qs (quarterly reports) that companies have to file with the agency. All publicly traded U.S. firms are now required to post their financial data electronically. Investors also are eager readers of 13Ds, the form shareholders have to file when they buy more than 5% of a company's shares. If you search for all 13D filings submitted during the past 90 days, you'll get a free list of companies that could include many potential takeover targets. Note, however, that a bill introduced in Congress would privatize the database, turning it into a pay service. Address: http://www.sec.gov.

Wall Street Journal's Money & Investing Update. Night owls who tap into this site after midnight eastern time can read the What's News summary from the front page of the next day's *Journal* hours before the newspaper hits the streets. Better yet, big business stories with lots of breaking news are updated throughout the day. Address: http://update.wsj.com.

Calculating your funds' results. Keeping current on your fund portfolio's value is a simple chore for your computer but a valuable one for you, especially if you own funds from several families and reinvest dividends and gains. To track your portfolio, the computer fetches up-to-date price quotes via modem for each of your funds and then totals up your holdings. The noncomputer alternative is to go through newspaper listings and multiply each fund's closing price by the number of shares you own. Without these periodic updates, you don't know your portfolio's exact value (which may be eye-opening in itself). You can't be sure whether you have a gain or a loss on any individual fund (which affects your tax strategy). Most important, you can't tell whether your portfolio still conforms to the asset allocation you intended.

The quickest way to get tracking is to open an account with one of the big online services like America Online, Compuserve or Prodigy. All three offer portfolio update services as part of their basic monthly charge. Of the three, we prefer the simplicity of America Online. From its Quotes & Portfolios menu, you can find the latest price for any of more than 5,000 funds simply by entering the investment's name or ticker symbol. Once the quote appears on your screen, you can click a button titled "add to portfolio" to append it to a ledger of 100 issues. Thereafter, whenever you open your portfolio the computer automatically will show the latest price for each item plus the overall value of your holdings and your loss or gain.

If you're serious about following your fund portfolio by computer, however, the online services won't satisfy you for long. They make no provision for reinvested dividends. You have to create a separate portfolio entry for each purchase. A dedicated fund investor will probably be happier with personal finance software such as Quicken, Managing Your Money and Wealth Builder (800-346-2024). All three allow you to hook up with online information sources to download daily quotes, and all let you organize the data more or less as you want it. For example, Quicken, the biggest seller of the three, lets you create separate portfolios for your various accounts—IRA, 401(k) and so forth. It handles reinvested dividends and gains with ease. It produces written reports or graphs of your investment performance. And when you sell, it supplies the data you need to complete Schedule D, the tax form for reporting capital losses or gains. You can also transfer the data from Quicken (or from any of its main competitors) to most popular tax preparation programs.

There is one main drawback to tracking your portfolio on Quicken or its brethren. If you want the program to calculate the tax cost of funds you already own, you'll have to enter your transaction history manually, which could take hours. If you would rather not bother, try calling the fund companies where you have accounts and asking them to compute the average cost of your shares. Then enter the number of shares you own and their average cost as your opening balance for each new fund account. Henceforth, you can record reinvested dividends and capital gains normally. The program keeps an accurate tally of your tax basis provided you use the average cost method of calculating your basis as well as your gain or loss.

Picking funds on your computer. Suppose that you are looking for a good small-cap growth fund with stable management, low expenses and a history of above-average gains at below-average risk. You have two choices. You can camp out in the library and comb through financial publications looking for that special fund. Or you could let your computer search quickly through nearly all of today's fund names and find the handful that qualify. Computer screening programs, which allow you to sift through a large database of funds to locate those that fit your precise needs, have elevated fund picking from a shot in the dark to an almost scientific endeavor. Once only mainframes had the power to handle screens. Now at least a dozen screening programs costing anywhere from $25 to $290 run contentedly on late-model home PCs.

Which program performs best? The answer hinges largely on how much you already know about funds. If you think 12b-1 is a vitamin, for example, you will want to stick with programs geared for novices, such as Intuit's Your Mutual Fund Selector. This program, available as a CD-ROM or bundled free with Quicken Deluxe, begins by interviewing you to determine your assets, goals and risk tolerance. It then produces a pie chart showing how you should divide your money among various types of funds and even recommends specific buys from its fund database. There's also a primer on fund investing, where you can find out that 12b-1 is an annual marketing fee.

With Selector, even someone who knows nothing about investing can put together a respectable portfolio. If you plugged in information on a hypothetical 30-year old couple who wanted to save for their child's college education, the program suggests that they put 30% of their money in growth-stock funds, 14% in overseas stock funds, 33% in bond funds and the rest in U.S. Treasury bills. That's a reasonable mix for cautious investors. Experienced investors may find parts of Selector a bit silly, however. One video clip features a smirking croupier who deals you a hand of blackjack in a test designed to measure your appetite for risk. A more serious drawback is that the program can screen funds based on only 10 criteria, some of which are of dubious value.

If you would rather work with a wider universe of fund possibilities, check out the software packages from Morningstar, the Chicago fund research firm (800-735-0700). Morningstar's Ascent and Principia Plus programs are designed for serious fund pickers and allow you to roam a database that includes roughly a hundred items of information on more than 6,000 funds. Another competent screening program is Wealth Builder from Reality Online. This product includes an excellent portfolio tracking feature and a database of funds supplied by Morningstar that you can update online daily. It also aspires to be a complete financial planning package, covering stocks, bonds, money markets and CDs.

The principal drawback to these screening programs (except for Selector) is that you need to know what to screen for. If you don't, but would like to learn, try joining an investment club that focuses on computer users. The American Association of Individual Investors sponsors many such groups. It also publishes a bimonthly newsletter, *Computerized Investing* (800-428-2244), that reviews investing software and online services.

6

Rating Today's 25 Largest Funds

The 15 Largest Stock Funds

Just how big are America's 15 beefiest stock funds? (We rate the 10 biggest bond funds starting on page 168.) In total, the 15 boast combined assets of nearly $300 billion, according to Morningstar. Chances are, you own one or more of them now or may find yourself considering one of them in the future. Popularity and performance don't always go hand in hand, of course. To find out just how good these giants are, we dissected portfolios, quizzed fund managers and talked to fund analysts. Our buy, hold and pass recommendations appear below.

MONEY believes a long-term program of steady investment in topnotch funds, anchored by index funds, is the best way to reach your financial goals. Thus we base our ratings on more than just our short-term outlook for the year ahead. We also consider the soundness of each fund's strategy, its long-term record, management continuity and expenses. We put a hold on nine of the 15 stock funds, including No. 1 megafund Fidelity Magellan and No. 4 Fidelity Puritan. Both are difficult to rate now as a result of having recently installed new fund managers in Fidelity's latest organizational makeover. In other instances we assigned a hold where we conclude index funds are a better choice. Six portfolios, including EuroPacific Growth, Janus Fund and Vanguard Windsor, earn our buy sign. That means you should feel confident opening an account or adding to an existing one. In our view, these outstanding performers figure to post above-average returns this year and beyond. The latest data on performance and expenses for all 15 heavyweights can be found in the fund rankings that accompany this guide.

Hold **Fidelity Magellan.** For the third time in six years, investors in the nation's largest mutual fund, $55 billion Fidelity Magellan, must decide whether to entrust their money to a new manager. This time, the fresh face is Fidelity ace Robert Stansky, who moves into the hot seat vacated in May when Jeff Vinik quit suddenly after four years to start his own money management firm. So far Fidelity reports that the owners of Magellan aren't following Vinik out the door. That loyalty seems justified to the investment advisers that we interviewed. Their advice? Magellan shareholders have no reason to flee. And keep contributing if you have Magellan in your 401(k) plan (three out of every four Magellan dollars now come from retirement accounts). New investors, however, should pass on Magellan.

Here's why you can stick with Magellan. "Even with its size, the fund has managed to beat the market over the long term," says San Francisco investment adviser Kurt Brouwer. "And sponsor Fidelity is going to put all its resources into making sure it succeeds." Moreover, Stansky demonstrated plenty of stock market smarts in his nine-year stint at Fidelity Growth Company. His focus on firms posting revenue gains of at least 10% to 15% a year generated a 16% annual return during his tenure, beating both the S&P 500 index's 13% gain and Magellan's 14% advance. Morningstar's Don Phillips believes Stansky's taste for large stocks will give him an edge. Says he: "I think Stansky will have an easier time running Magellan than did Vinik, whose clear preference for small and mid-size companies made for difficult maneuvering." As impressive as Stansky's credentials are, people looking for a new place to park their money should probably avoid Magellan. There are simply too many attractive alternatives that don't have the disadvantages of Magellan's gargantuan size. Let's face it; the portfolio has changed dramatically since the days when it was run by fund star Peter Lynch. Most notably, the world's biggest fund has quadrupled in size from about $13 billion in 1990, the year Lynch ended his 13-year tenure.

Hold _Investment Company of America._ No fewer than eight portfolio managers labor to pick stocks for $28 billion Investment Company of America, one of several entries on our list from the American Funds group. But that crowded kitchen cooks up some pretty bland broth. According to Morningstar, about 95% of ICA's performance can be attributed to the performance of the S&P 500 index. And when measured against no-load Vanguard's Index 500 fund, profiled below, ICA comes up short. Over a recent five-year period, ICA's 14% annual return lagged the Index 500's 16% advance. And when ICA's hefty 5.75% load is factored into the equation, its five-year return lags even more. Risk management is one area where ICA shines, however. ICA has registered about 30% less volatility (according to Morningstar's proprietary risk measure) than stock funds as a group during the past decade. By comparison, Index 500's 10-year risk score is about 15% below the norm for stock funds. Adding it all up, investors have no reason to bail out of ICA. But if you're looking to put new money to work in a large-stock fund, you're better off with the index portfolio, making ICA a hold.

Buy _Vanguard Index 500._ Last year was a vintage one for the S&P 500 and the $22 billion Vanguard index fund that shadows it. The portfolio's 37% gain beat roughly 65% of all U.S. stock funds, and its long-term record is even better. In the past 10 years, the fund has returned nearly 14% annually. Comparatively few U.S. stock funds can boast higher numbers. There are no secrets to the fund's success. Its holdings mirror the S&P 500 index, and its annual expenses are a scant 0.2% of assets. Alarmed by last year's euphoria, manager Gus Sauter wants shareholders to brace themselves for slower growth. "It is irrational to expect 10% to 15% annual returns on a regular basis in the future," he warns. Still, the Vanguard Index 500 figures to top most actively managed funds over the long term. That makes it a desirable core holding for practically any fund portfolio, not to mention a strong buy again this year.

Hold *Washington Mutual Investors.* Owning shares in $21 billion Washington Mutual is far from a capital offense, as its three-year, five-year and 10-year returns rank within the top third of growth and income funds. Yet, like ICA, its American Funds family sibling, this team-managed portfolio talks, walks and acts a lot like an index fund. While Washington Mutual's eight managers have a decidedly value-oriented approach to stock picking, 95% of the portfolio is invested in S&P 500 stocks. During a recent five-year span, Washington Mutual's 16% annual return did slightly outpace the gain of no-load Vanguard Index 500. But shareholders earned less after paying the 5.75% sales levy. In effect, you're paying managers to track the S&P 500 index—albeit with slightly less volatility than the Vanguard fund. "It's hard to make a huge argument for Washington Mutual over an index fund," says Morningstar analyst Laura Lallos, and we agree. If you're in it, stay there. If not, look elsewhere.

Hold *Fidelity Contrafund.* When we bestowed a buy rating on $19 billion Contrafund last year, it held a reasonable 22% stake in technology issues. Then manager Will Danoff began snapping up computer and telecom stocks with both hands, nearly doubling their share of the fund to 40% by mid-1995. The big rally in technology stocks helped Contra return an impressive 30% in 1995, showing that Danoff has a knack for moving in and out of market sectors at the right time. He lately has pared his tech position, though not enough to change the fact that the fund is a bit risky, in our view, for most investors. If you're in it, hold. If not, pass.

Buy *Fidelity Growth & Income.* Manager Steven Kaye, who has been at the helm of this $19 billion fund

(3% load) since 1993, recently had large bets on the healthcare sector. That's been good medicine. Over a recent three-year period, the fund ranked in the top 10% of its category with 45% less volatility than its peers. Finance and consumer staples also account for big slices of the portfolio, while technology issues claim only a small share. That recipe should serve this conservative fund well in the year ahead, prompting us to upgrade it to a buy from last year's hold.

Hold *Twentieth Century Ultra.* "Being aggressive pays off over time," says James Stowers, one of Ultra's three managers. Sure does. Investors willing to buy $18 billion Ultra and hold on tight have enjoyed a five-year return of 20% annually, vs. 16% for the S&P 500. Even so, last year we mustered only enough enthusiasm to rate the fund a hold. Subpar performance in two of the prior three years, coupled with a threefold increase in assets since 1991, made us question whether this fund could still produce sizzling performance, as it did when it climbed 37% in 1989 and 87% in 1991. The answer was yes, largely because of the boom in tech stocks. They recently still commanded a big chunk of assets. Our advice is merely to hang on to what you've got. The fund seems too risky to merit additional funds from most investors. If your sights are firmly fixed on the long term, we can't argue too much if you take a deep breath and buy some Ultra shares. The fund has richly rewarded risk-takers.

Hold *Fidelity Puritan.* Rich Fentin, who has piloted $17 billion Puritan since 1987, was replaced this year by colleague Bettina Doulton, formerly manager of several Fidelity funds including $6.9 billion Value (now run by Fentin). We think it's too early to assess Doulton's potential impact on the fund's lately tepid performance. Thus Puritan ranks no better than a hold.

Buy *Vanguard Windsor.* The big question facing Windsor holders is what happens now that John Neff, a grand master of value investing, has retired from running the $15 billion fund. (Since Windsor is closed to new investors, only current account holders can buy shares.) Neff's singular skill at spotting undervalued companies helped him compile a most remarkable record of earning 14% annually over the past 31 years, vs. 10% for the S&P 500. And we continue to rate Windsor a buy under new manager Charles Freeman, who took over this year. Freeman has spent his entire 25-year career at Neff's elbow. "We have a tried and true way of going about our business, and that will continue," says Freeman. What sets Freeman and Neff apart from other bargain hunters is their bold bets on shares they deem underpriced. "When we have a good idea, we run with it," says Freeman. "Typically, 35% to 40% or more of the fund is in the largest 10 holdings." Windsor lately was deep into financial services, commodities, energy and automakers. The portfolio was also flush with cash, giving Freeman a bankroll that he is eager to put to work. Speaking of himself and the fund's four analysts, Freeman says: "The Neff disciples are ready to go forward."

Hold *Income Fund of America.* Investing mostly in large-cap stocks and bonds, IFA's six-member management team has produced five- and 10-year returns that rank in the top third of the balanced fund category. That solid showing earns the $15 billion fund (5.75% load) its second straight hold rating. The fund buys large-cap value stocks and keeps a third of its bond stake in riskier issues rated below investment grade, contributing to its hefty 5% yield. And its volatility is roughly 50% below that of similar income-oriented stock funds. Nevertheless, we think investors looking for a fund that holds both stocks and bonds can get better results with no-load Lindner Dividend.

Buy *Janus Fund.* This $14 billion no-load portfolio, managed by James Craig, earns another buy recommendation. While its performance figures hover close to those of Vanguard Index 500 fund, Janus isn't an S&P

500 clone. One third of assets recently were invested in smaller-cap or foreign issues, including European shares, which Craig figures will blossom in 1996. Unlike an index fund that stays fully invested, Craig seeks cover in cash when he gets nervous. These days, however, he's brimming with confidence. Hot technology stocks represent a modest portion of assets. "Craig is a good stock picker who does a great job of managing risk," says Larry Chin of the newsletter *No-Load Fund Analyst*. That makes Janus a good match for conservative growth-stock investors.

Hold Vanguard Wellington.

Vincent Bajakian, who was Wellington's main manager for 23 years, was killed late last year when the private plane he was piloting crashed. Succeeding Bajakian is Ernst von Metzsch, who runs the stock portion of this $14 billion no-load. Paul Kaplan continues to oversee fixed-income investments. Von Metzsch, who started working with Bajakian in 1976, plans no changes in the fund's conservative strategy. Wellington typically allocates 60% to 70% of its assets to common stocks, with an emphasis on blue-chip issues, and the remainder to high-quality corporate bonds and U.S. Government securities. "The approach Vincent took as an investor is one I shared, and there is not going to be a change in style or emphasis," says von Metzsch. His first challenge is to sustain the solid performance achieved with the help of Bajakian's prescient plays in the financial sector. There is no reason to think von Metzsch can't keep up the pace. But since he is new to the job, Wellington warrants a hold for now.

Buy Fidelity Equity Income II.

One point we didn't make in our earlier assessment of this large-cap value fund (profiled on page 38) concerns its runaway growth. In the past 18 months, Fidelity Equity Income II's assets have almost doubled to $14 billion. And why not? Manager Brian Posner's three-year return of 15% annually has handily beat the 10% annual gain of his peers and ranks in the top 5% of the total return category. Even better, he has achieved those results with less volatility than the norm for stock funds. A strict value investor, Posner largely avoids technology stocks that typically sport high earnings multiples. Instead, the fund has been heavily invested in financial and energy services companies. Posner's style and record indicate that this fund might be a particularly smart choice for what figures to be a challenging year ahead. "If you're looking for a single, well-diversified fund that won't kill you in a down market, this is it," says Eric Kobren of Insight Group in Wellesley, Mass. We rate the fund a solid buy.

Buy **EuroPacific Growth.** Its team of five portfolio managers handle their foreign stock picking with the aplomb of seasoned diplomats, landing among the top international funds for the past three, five and 10 years. Despite its 5.75% load, the $13 billion fund remains a strong buy for investors seeking global diversification. The portfolio seems well positioned to benefit from the widely anticipated rebound in European markets this year. Nearly half the portfolio is nestled in European blue chips such as food giant Nestlé, drugmaker Sandoz and automaker Daimler-Benz.

Hold **Fidelity Asset Manager.** Bob Beckwitt produced outstanding results from 1990 through 1993 by nimbly steering this $11 billion asset-allocation fund in and out of stocks, bonds, cash and foreign markets. But his more recent moves have not been so deft. Caught with a stiff 15% stake in Mexican stocks when the peso was devalued, the fund sank 7% in 1994, vs. a 1% gain for the S&P 500. Then Beckwitt turned wary, building up a cash stake that recently was almost a third of his portfolio. That excessive caution left him sitting in the stands during last year's spectacular stock and bond rallies. These missteps prompted Fidelity to replace Beckwitt this year with colleague Richard Habermann, who was overseeing the company's international investments. We think it's too soon to assess Habermann's impact on the fund, which in our view rates no higher than a hold.

The 10 Biggest Bond Funds

Among these behemoths, only Vanguard's cost-conscious Fixed Income GNMA and Municipal Intermediate earned MONEY's buy ratings for reasons explained below. In four cases, we placed holds on high-cost bond funds mainly because very similar low-cost alternatives were readily available, usually from Vanguard, which makes a fetish of keeping costs down. And we stamped a sell on two chronic underperformers, Dean Witter U.S. Government Securities and Dreyfus Municipal Bond.

Hold **Franklin U.S. Government.** Managers Jack Lemein, Roger Bayston and Tony Coffey have made consistency the hallmark of the country's largest bond fund (4.25% load). Their strategy is to buy and hold mortgage-backed bonds, called Ginnie Maes. They look for the highest yields they can find and completely avoid derivatives, those tricky securities that rained losses on many bond funds when rates rose during 1994. "I don't want to add unnecessary risk to the portfolio by doing anything flagrantly speculative," says Lemein. The $10 billion fund recently yielded 7.3%, among the highest in its category. Despite those impressive numbers, we rate this fund a hold because a superior alternative is readily available for investors not already in the fund. Vanguard GNMA (see below) pursues a similar strategy but levies no sales charge and has posted better numbers for the past three, five and 10 years.

Sell **Dean Witter U.S. Government.** To be fair, manager Rajesh Gupta has breathed some life into this lackluster $7 billion fund since taking over in 1992. During the past three years, the fund's 4.1% annual return hasn't lagged far behind the 4.7% of the typical taxable bond fund. About 70% of the fund is usually in Ginnie Maes, 25% in Treasuries and the rest in other government securities. Nevertheless, Gupta remains handicapped by the fund's 1.2% annual expense ratio, which is above the 1% average for bond funds. (The fund also has a 5% deferred sales charge, or exit fee, that phases out over six years.) Since there are similar funds with much lower expenses and better records, this one warrants a sell.

Hold *Franklin Federal Tax-Free.* Manager Andy Jennings has piloted this $7 billion long-term muni fund (4.25% load) to sterling returns of 7.8% annually over the past five years, vs. 7.3% for the typical muni fund. And the portfolio's juicy 6.3% yield is among the highest in the group. Jennings believes the best buys are bonds maturing in 20 to 25 years. He especially likes insured California bonds that have fallen in price since the Orange County bankruptcy. While we consider this fund topnotch, we can't rate it higher than hold. Our reason is that investors can get better results without paying a sales charge from Vanguard Muni Long Term, which has produced a higher return than the Franklin fund over the past one, three, five and 10 years.

Buy *Vanguard Fixed Income GNMA.* Thanks to Vanguard's ultralow expenses and a plain-vanilla strategy of buying mortgage-backed securities at face value, this $7 billion fund has landed in the top 1% of its category for the past five, 10 and 15 years. Few funds of any kind can make that claim. GNMA funds do best when rates are stable. When rates fall, homeowners tend to repay their mortgages faster, depriving Ginnie Mae holders of the appreciation other bondholders enjoy. And stability is what fund manager Paul Kaplan sees ahead. "So our strategy is to own bonds that get a lot of yield," says Kaplan. The only objection we can raise against this fund is that taxable bond investors will get almost identical results, with roughly the same subpar volatility, by buying an index fund that mimics the Lehman Bros. aggregate bond index.

Hold *Bond Fund of America.* At first glance, the performance of this $6 billion fund seems unassailable. Even after accounting for its 4.75% sales charge, it manages to outpoint the leading taxable bond index fund, Vanguard Bond Index Total Bond Market. But that edge came with 20% more volatility than the index fund. BFA also stumbled badly in the bond rout of 1994, losing 7% from February to December of that year, while the index fund slipped 5%. Moreover, we're uncomfortable with BFA's dabbling in derivatives, which contributed to losses in 1994. Thus we rate the fund as a hold.

Hold IDS High-Yield Tax-Exempt. Manager Kurt Larson, in charge since 1979, has made enough savvy moves lately to persuade us to upgrade this $6 billion fund to hold from sell. His major coup was correctly anticipating last year's bond rally by buying longer-term securities that get the biggest lift from falling rates. That helped the fund land in the top 30% of its category. To boost yield, recently 6%, Larson invests a chunk of the fund's assets in muni junk bonds rated below investment grade. In contrast, the typical high-yield muni fund carries a smaller junk stake. While the fund's performance has improved, its pesky 5% sales charge is still a major drawback. Hence we can rate it no higher than a hold for current shareholders. New investors looking for high tax-free yields from a no-load fund should consider T. Rowe Price's Tax Free High-Yield.

Buy Vanguard Municipal Intermediate. Ian MacKinnon, Vanguard's bond chief, was caught off guard by last year's bond boom. "We trimmed our sails in 1995, and our duration was too short for the rally," he says. (Duration indicates a fund's sensitivity to rate swings.) Still, this $5 billion entry remains a buy for its superb long-term record and tiny fees. Over five years the fund has beaten most of its peers, and its expense ratio of 0.2% is well below the group average of 0.8%. The prospect of tax reforms have widened the usual price gap between munis and Treasuries. So managers MacKinnon and Chris Ryon have made a double-barrel bet, buying muni futures contracts and selling Treasury bonds short. That move will pay off if markets return to

their customary alignment and should help restore the fund to its customary position—leading the muni pack.

Hold Kemper U.S. Government. Under the leadership of Paul Sloan, who took over in May 1995, this fund is turning in a performance reminiscent of its 1980s glory days. Sloan aggressively shuffles the $4 billion fund (4.5% load) to make the most of market movements. For example, he made a good call ahead of last year's bond rally by selling mortgage-backed securities and buying Treasuries, which get more of a lift from falling rates. But given his short tenure, it is too soon to tell whether he can continue to outguess the crowd. Therefore, the fund warrants a hold.

Sell Dreyfus Municipal Bond. That's our verdict on this no-load, managed by Richard Moynihan since 1976. The evidence still points to rival funds, such as previously profiled Vanguard Muni Intermediate, as superior choices for long-term investors. The Vanguard fund's three-year and five-year performance outpaces this $4 billion Dreyfus portfolio. Moreover, the Vanguard fund subjected its shareholders to less volatility than the typical muni fund during those periods. The Dreyfus fund was more volatile over the past three and five years. Further, in the bond market's 1994 sell-off, the Dreyfus fund tumbled an alarming 10% while Vanguard Muni Intermediate slid a less painful 5%. Why get white knuckles holding on? We say sell.

Hold Kemper Municipal Bond. A newcomer to our list, this $3 billion fund (4.5% load) has benefited lately from manager Christopher Mier's ability to adjust the portfolio ahead of changing interest rates. But like many bond funds that levy sales fees, this one suffers in comparison with a no-load, low-expense Vanguard entry. Again, it's Vanguard's Muni Intermediate, which has produced similar returns over the past one, five and 10 years, while subjecting shareholders to less volatility than the Kemper fund.

Glossary

Aggressive growth fund. One that strives for maximum capital gains, as opposed to current income, from stocks that are expected to appreciate faster than the market.

Asset allocation fund. These funds spread their assets among a variety of investments such as U.S. stocks, foreign stocks, precious metals and bonds, altering the mix in an effort to time markets and enhance returns.

Back-end load. See **Redemption fees**.

Balanced fund. An income-oriented portfolio that typically has an even-handed mix of bonds and stocks (including convertibles).

Certificate of deposit (CD). Debt instrument, issued by financial institutions, that usually pays interest.

Closed-end fund. Unlike conventional open-end funds, which continually buy and sell their shares at net asset value, closed-end funds have a fixed number of shares that trade the way stocks do on exchanges.

Convertible. Corporate bond or preferred stock that is exchangeable for a set number of common shares at a prestated price.

Credit rating. Evaluation of debt securities' credit risk, or likelihood of default, by rating services such as Moody's Investors Service and Standard & Poor's Corporation.

Diversification. The spreading of one's risk by investing in a wide range of securities.

Dividend. Distribution of earnings to shareholders. Fund dividends are paid out of income generated by stocks and bonds in the portfolio, usually on a quarterly basis.

Dollar cost averaging. Installment purchase technique that involves investing a fixed amount of money in stocks or mutual fund shares at regular intervals, such as monthly or quarterly, rather than all at once. The objective of this strategy is to buy fewer shares when prices are high and more shares when they are low.

Exchange privilege. An option enabling fund shareholders to transfer their investment from one fund to another within the same fund family, as their needs or objectives change. Funds typically allow investors to use the exchange privilege several times a year for free or for a low fee.

Ex-dividend. Period between the announcement and the payment of a mutual fund's next dividend. An investor who buys shares during that interval is not entitled to the dividend. A fund that has gone ex-dividend is marked with an "x" in newspaper listings.

Exit fee. See **Redemption fees**.

Expense ratio. Amount, expressed as a percentage of total assets, that shareholders paid in the past year for mutual fund operating expenses and management fees.

Front-end load. See **Load**.

Ginnie Mae. The nickname for the federally backed debt securities issued by the GNMA (Government National Mortgage Association). Ginnie Maes represent a pool of mortgages; investors receive the homeowners' payments of interest and principal.

Growth fund. One whose main objective is capital appreciation by investing in stocks that are expected to increase steadily in value over time.

Growth stock. Share in an expanding company that has reported above-average earnings gains over the last few years and is expected to maintain or increase its growth rate in the years ahead.

Hedge. A defensive investment strategy, often involving the buying or selling of options, to offset possible losses and thereby to reduce risk.

Income fund. A portfolio that is managed to generate steady income rather than capital gains from bonds, high-dividend stocks and other income-producing securities.

Index fund. One whose portfolio closely duplicates that of an index such as the Standard & Poor's 500-stock index and whose performance therefore mirrors that of the market overall.

Individual Retirement Account (IRA). Personal retirement account that an employed person may be entitled to fund with tax-deductible contributions of up to $2000 per year ($2250 a year for a couple with a nonworking spouse). You can fully deduct your contribution if you are not covered by a pension plan or if you earn less than $25,000 (single) or $40,000 (married and filing jointly). All earnings generated in the account accumulate tax-deferred until the funds are withdrawn. Early withdrawals (those made before age 59.5) are subject to a 10% tax penalty and income taxes.

Junk bond. A high-yielding bond with a speculative credit rating (BB or lower grading, for example, by Standard & Poor's) that reflects doubts about the issuing company's or government's credit strength.

Load. Commission or sales charge for buying fund shares through a broker, financial planner or insurance agent. Some funds that sell directly to the public also charge loads. Funds that do not are called no-load funds.

Management fee. Charge against investor assets to cover the costs of managing the portfolio of a mutual fund. The fee is a fixed percentage of the fund's assets and is disclosed in the fund's prospectus.

Market timing. A strategy of buying or selling securities, including fund shares, to take advantage of (or reduce one's exposure to) anticipated changes in market conditions. For example, fund shareholders might switch from a stock fund to a short-term bond or money-market fund when they think the stock market is about to fall.

Maturity. The date on which a bond's principal becomes due and payable.

Money-market fund. One that invests in short-term government securities, bank certificates of deposit and other low-risk, low-return securities. These funds pay so-called money market rates of interest, and withdrawals from them can be made anytime at a predictable per-share value.

Municipal bond. Bond issued by a state or local government. In most cases, the interest paid is exempt from federal taxes and, if the bondholder lives in the state where the bond was issued, from state and local taxes too.

Net asset value (NAV). The value of a share of a mutual fund. A fund computes its NAV daily by taking the closing prices of securities in its portfolio, adding the value of other assets such as cash, subtracting the fund's liabilities, and dividing the result by the number of shares outstanding.

Operating expenses. The normal costs a mutual fund incurs in conducting business, such as the expenses associated with maintaining offices, staff and equipment. There are also expenses related to maintaining the fund's portfolio of securities. These expenses are paid from the fund's assets before any earnings are distributed to shareholders.

Option. An agreement that gives the buyer the right to buy (call option) or sell (put option) 100 shares of a particular stock or stock index at a fixed price during a preset period. An option produces income, called a premium, for the seller, who in exchange gives up ownership of the securities in the event the option buyer exercises his right.

PE. See **Price-earnings ratio**.

Portfolio turnover. A measure, usually expressed in annual terms, of how frequently a fund's manager trades in and out of the securities in the fund.

Preferred stock. A class of stock that pays a fixed dividend and has preference over common stock in the payment of dividends and the liquidation of the issuing company's assets. Preferred stockholders do not normally have voting rights.

Price-earnings ratio (PE). Also known as the earnings multiple, it gives investors an idea of how much they are paying for a stock's earnings or a fund's portfolio. The ratio is figured by dividing a stock's price by its earnings per share as reported over the past 12 months or forecast in future years by analysts who follow the company. The higher the PE, the higher the profit growth investors expect in the future.

Prospectus. The official document that a mutual fund supplies to all prospective shareholders, identifying the fund's management company, outlining its investment objectives and assessing the risks involved. A corollary document, called Part B or the statement of additional information, provides greater details on subjects such as fees.

Redeem. To cash in your shares by selling them back to the mutual fund. Shares may be redeemed on any business day.

Redemption fees. Often called exit fees or back-end loads, they are deducted from money you take out of some funds when you redeem, or sell, shares. Some exit fees, which can be as high as 1% of the amount redeemed, decline to zero over a period of a few months or years; others remain constant. Back-end loads, also known as contingent deferred sales charges, typically are levied by load funds that do not have initial, or front-end, sales charges. The loads start at 4% to 6% on withdrawals during your first year in the fund and gradually decline to zero over four to six years.

Reinvestment privilege. An option that's available to fund shareholders in which dis-

tributions of dividends and capital gains are automatically turned back into the fund to buy new shares and thus increase holdings.

Single-state muni fund. One specializing in tax-exempt bonds of government agencies within a single state. Residents of that state receive income from the bonds that is free from state as well as federal taxes.

Specialty fund. Also called a sector fund, it restricts its holdings to companies in a particular industry, service or region.

Stable value account. Consists of contracts, issued by insurance companies or banks, that promise to pay a set rate of interest for a certain period of time, typically two to five years. The accounts usually pay interest rates that are a percentage point or more higher than those offered by money-market funds.

Standard & Poor's 500-stock index. A popular measurement of the stock market's performance based on prices of 500 widely held stocks traded in the U.S.

Total return. The dividends, interest and capital gains that a fund achieves over a given period of time.

Total return fund. One that pursues both growth and income by investing in a mix of high-yielding stocks and bonds.

12b-1 fees. Named after a Securities and Exchange Commission rule that permits them, these assessments against shareholders' assets are levied by many mutual funds to help pay for promotion expenses. Such 12b-1 fees are usually included in a fund's expense ratio.

Volatility. The degree to which securities such as mutual fund shares move up or down in price within a given period.

Yield. The dividend or interest income that a stock, bond or mutual fund share pays out in one year. Yield is expressed as a percentage of a stock's or bond's market price or a fund's net asset value per share.

Zero-coupon bond. A bond that makes no periodic interest payments but instead is sold at a discount from its face value. The buyer of a zero receives the rate of return by the gradual appreciation of the bond, which is redeemable at face value at maturity.

Index

Aggressive growth funds, 12, 18-9, 32, 42, 45, 65, 143
Asset allocation, 81-2, 84, 111
    for life's stages, 82-8
    for 401(k) funds, 107-13
Asset allocation funds, 81

Back-end load, 141
Balanced funds, 75, 83
Bond funds, 70, 77-80
    corporate, 79
    credit ratings, 77
    derivatives in, 129, 132, 170
    foreign, 80
    Government, 78
    junk bonds in, 77, 79
    mortgage-backed, 79
    municipal, 79
    rating the 10 largest, 168-71
    risks of, 70
Bond market forecast, 15, 35-6, 52

Capital gains
    distributions of, 11, 142, 149
    as fund profits, 150
    reinvestment of, 11, 146-50
Commissions, 66, 142
Contingent deferred sales charge, 141
Convertible bonds, 75
Corporate bond funds, 79

Computer-aided investing
    software, 151-3, 156-8
    online services, 152-6

Derivatives, 129, 132, 170
Distributions
    options for, 146
    tax liability for, 146
Dividends, 77, 147
Dollar's value abroad, 21, 74
Dollar cost averaging, 88
    constant ratio planning, 92
    value averaging, 90
    variable installment, 92
Dow Jones industrial average
    outlook for, 15, 36, 53

Ex-dividend, 147
Expense ratio of funds, 16, 134, 141

Federal Reserve, 13, 34
Fees and expenses of funds, 11, 16, 106-7, 140
Foreign currency swings, 21-2, 80
Foreign regional funds, 73
Foreign funds, **See** Overseas funds
401(k) funds
    expenses of, 106-7
    investing strategies for, 99, 101, 108, 111

mistakes to avoid, 119
rollovers, 120
taxes on, 96, 118, 123
withdrawals from, 98, 113, 117,
   121, 125
Front-end load, 20, 141

Ginnie Maes, 79
Global funds, 73
Gold
   as inflation hedge, 19
   funds that invest in, 70
Government bond funds, 78
Growth and income, **See** Total
   return funds
Growth funds, 19, 39, 58-60, 72

Income funds, **See** Bond funds
Index funds, 56-7
Inflation, 13, 34, 54
IRAs
   rollovers to, 98, 120, 122
   withdrawals from, 125
Initial sales charge, **See** Front-end
   load
Interest rates, 14
   and bond prices, 15, 34, 52, 78
Interest rate risk, 64
Intermediate-term bond funds, 78
International funds, 21, 73
Investing styles, 63

Junk bonds, 19
   in corporate bond funds, 77, 79

Load, 20, 66, 134, 137, 141
Long-term bond funds, 36, 78
Losses, 65, 150
Low-load funds, 66

Managers of funds
   and investing strategies, 28-9, 71
   effect on performance, 144-5
Market timing, 73
Municipal bond funds, 20
   tax-exemption of, 20, 79
   types of, 79

Net asset value (NAV), 135
New funds, 41-5
No-load funds. **See** Load

Overseas funds, 73-5

Per-share data, 143
Political risk, 64
Portfolio turnover rate, 142
Prospectus
   how to read, 143

Real estate
   investing in, 70
Regional funds, 73
Retirement plans, 114
Risk, 64, 66-70
   currency, 67, 74, 80
   interest rate, 64
   political, 64

Securities and Exchange
   Commission, 27, 136
Short-term bond funds, 78
Single-country funds, 73
Single-state muni funds, 20, 80
Size of fund
   importance of, 22-30
Small-company stock funds, 17, 46-
   7, 71
Stable value account, 102, 108, 110
Stock funds, 67
   big vs. small, 22-7
   foreign, 21, 67, 73-4
   rating the 15 largest, 160-7
   risks of, 67
   styles of, 71

Tax computation methods, 151
Taxable gains, 149
Taxes and 401(k)s, 118-26
Total return funds, 75
   average weighted maturity, 76
   credit quality, 76
   performance of, 76
   types of, 76
Treasury bills, 88
Treasury bonds, 78
12b-1 fees, 142

Value funds, 38, 41, 72, 86
Volatility, 35

Withdrawals
   and back-end loads, 141
   and taxes. 150-1